Pathways of
Police Misconduct

PATHWAYS OF POLICE MISCONDUCT

Problem Behavior Patterns and Trajectories from Two Cohorts

Christopher J. Harris
UNIVERSITY OF MASSACHUSETTS LOWELL

CAROLINA ACADEMIC PRESS
Durham, North Carolina

Library of Congress Cataloging-in-Publication Data

Harris, Christopher J.
Pathways of police misconduct : problem behavior patterns and
trajectories from two cohorts / Christopher J. Harris.
    p. cm.
Includes bibliographical references and index.
ISBN 978-1-59460-632-8 (alk. paper)
1. Police misconduct. 2. Police--Complaints against. I. Title.
HV7936.C56H37 2009
364.1'32--dc22

                                2009028661

CAROLINA ACADEMIC PRESS
700 Kent Street
Durham, North Carolina 27701
Telephone (919) 489-7486
Fax (919) 493-5668
www.cap-press.com

Printed in the United States of America

For my wife, Kathy

Contents

Acknowledgments

This work was written for two primary reasons. One is that I enjoy research in both policing and in life-course criminology, even though I consider myself a police scholar first and foremost. The second is that I was fortunate enough to work for Rob Worden on his very ambitious and well designed Early Intervention System (EIS) project, as this research is a secondary analysis of his project's data. The combination of both interest and opportunity rather serendipitously lead to the idea for this book. Since no work is truly written alone, there are many I owe thanks.

Research Site. Unfortunately, since this project was done in collaboration with a research site which wishes to remain anonymous, some of the people I would like to thank must also remain so. The head of the police department receives my admiration, since few would allow researchers into an agency to collect data on such sensitive issues as personnel complaints, civil litigation, uses of force, and the like. Such an undertaking does not happen without a progressive leader who is sincerely interested in improving the performance of his agency. I would also like to thank Sergeant Mary for helping us with data collection. Without her aid and skill, the data collection for the EIS project would have taken much longer.

EIS Project Staff. I had the esteemed pleasure of working alongside both Shelagh Catlin-Dorn and Shelley Schlief, both of whom are wonderful, intelligent people whose company on the project made the work that much more enjoyable. They were supportive of my effort in writing this book, and I owe both much thanks.

Colleagues. I owe Rob Worden a considerable debt, both for his allowing me to work on his project and the support and feedback he gave me in writing this book. David Bayley read and offered feedback and suggestions for this work, as did Terrance Thornberry, Hans Toch, and David McDowall. Jorge Chavez lent me his expertise with *Proc Traj*, and without it this work would have easily taken several more months. I have also received much support from the Criminal Justice faculty here at UMass Lowell. Thanks to all.

Home. My wife Kathy is my largest pillar of support. She provided encouragement when I despaired, incentive when I waned, and strength when I tired. Thanks would hardly be enough.

PATHWAYS OF
POLICE MISCONDUCT

Chapter 1

How Criminology Can Contribute to Understanding Police Misconduct

"In all these years as a cop I was always up to my ass in things that would turn your stomach and make your blood boil. But to me they don't mean anything but work. I might have lost my patience more often than I should have, but I am not proud of it. I have learned a long time ago that in this racket it is always better to be smart than to do things in ways that make you feel good in the moment. A lot of guys don't know that, and when they get to be forty years old and no longer feel like wrestling in the gutter with everybody who calls them a dirty son-of-a-bitch, they figure there is nothing left for them."

—A detective sergeant, as quoted by Bittner, *Functions of Police in Modern Society*

This quote by Bittner (1970) was used in his seminal work to emphasize an important point regarding the technical concerns of crime control—that officers should act in a calculated, informed manner and not on impulse. Acting on impulse forfeits the claim of practicing a profession, since at that moment police officers are acting no different than everyone else, ultimately degrading the occupation. No matter the justification, impulsive action is inefficient and uncontrollable, which obstructs the attainment of the officer's own interest. Such action might be an immediate source of emotional gratification, but, according to Bittner, it defeats every kind of other purpose the officer might have in mind. But the above quote also implies a deal more. It notes that officers take some time to learn this important lesson regarding crime control. How long it takes on average for officers to grasp this vital point is an interesting question, but it certainly would vary across the population of police officers. Youth and inexperience have long been thought to contribute to police violence and other problem behaviors and is something officers outgrow. This "John and Jane Wayne" syndrome has been seen as a developmental phase: after officers finish their initial probationary period, they enter their "adolescent phase," when they are the most dangerous to themselves and others. According to Meredith (1986), "This is the stage when you see [officers] wearing mirrored sunglasses and a carry a .44 magnum ... They spend time at home in front of a mirror, just practicing how to look like police officers" (p. 26). This phase lasts three to five years, after which officers presumably become more skilled and less problematic as they mature.

The quote above also implies that some officers do not learn this lesson; such officers continually act in ways that citizens, and perhaps administrators, might resent. These officers never seem to outgrow their "adolescent phase," or perhaps take an unusually long time to do so. Such officers are likely to have frequent problems in their contact with citizens, particularly resorting too quickly to their coercive authority, and perhaps even escalating situations where other, more skilled officers might have been successful in employing alternative tactics.

There have certainly been a number of well-publicized, and highly scrutinized, cases where officers acted impulsively, resulting in incidents of police violence. The beating of Rodney King at the hands of the Los Angeles Police Department (LAPD) is one of the most well-known of these types of incidents. Whether such incidents are extraordinarily rare, and hence why they are so widely publicized, or whether such incidents represent the proverbial "tip-of-the-iceberg" of the broader realm of police misconduct remains in question. But such a question cannot be answered with anecdotal evidence alone.

The subsequent investigation of the LAPD following the Rodney King incident by the Christopher Commission revealed much, but of particular interest here is the finding that 44 officers accounted for a disproportionate amount of citizen complaints filed alleging excessive force or improper police tactics. These officers, whom the Commission labeled *problem officers*, represented less than one-half of one percent of all the officers in the LAPD, but accounted for 15 percent of these types of citizen complaints. The Commission noted that this disproportion was not accounted for solely by the officers' assignment or arrest rates, implying these problem officers had a proclivity to use force too frequently and excessively (Independent Commission on the Los Angeles Police Department, 1991). Other research has also confirmed that a small percentage of officers account for a disproportionate amount of misconduct, measured through complaints filed by citizens, and has found that these problem officers tend to be predominately male, young, and inexperienced (Harris, 2009).

As a means of prospectively identifying problem officers and curtailing their behavior, some police administrators have employed a behavioral monitoring device called an Early Intervention System (EIS) which scans indicators of problem behaviors (e.g., citizen complaints, uses of force, police vehicle accidents), and flags employees who have surpassed some threshold on them (e.g., three citizen complaints in six months). Officers who are flagged are then subject to some form of intervention, and monitored thereafter to ensure problematic behaviors have been corrected. While this new technology is becoming more popular among police administrators, it is not yet known whether the implicit predictions upon which these systems are based have any validity,[1] largely because there is little information about problem officers or the continuity of problem behaviors more generally.

---

1. Only one study by Bazley, Mieczkowski, & Lersch (2009) examines this issue with regards to use of force indicators in EIS.

This book is designed to shed additional light on problem officers, but more importantly, places these problem officers within a larger framework that can examine the problematic behaviors of all police officers over the course of their careers. Most existing research on police work considers officers at only one point in time, making comparisons between officers, largely ignoring the changes within officers over their career course. If the younger, more inexperienced officers tend to be the most problematic, can anyone say with confidence that such officers will be continually problematic across the course of their careers? The detective sergeant quoted above seems to suggest that officers require time to properly acclimate to the police role, while others will be continually problematic. To properly investigate this notion, one needs to understand how experience shapes police behaviors that might be considered problematic, and develop a cohesive lexicon for characterizing these problem behaviors over police careers. As it stands, researchers have little knowledge of behavior patterns across officer careers in the aggregate, let alone a set of guidelines for examining an officer's longitudinal patterns of problem behavior more specifically.

As a means of gaining insight into police misconduct across careers, an analogous framework that examines antisocial behavior over time—the criminal career paradigm—is employed here.[2] This framework is relevant as it has outlined a way to organize key elements of deviant behavior throughout the life-course. The focus of this research will be the application of the criminal career framework, and a developmental perspective more generally, as a tool for understanding police officers' career paths in deviance over time. The application of such a framework will illustrate how incidents of problematic behavior are distributed across the police population, whether there are distinct types of career paths over time, and moreover, whether there exists a distinct subtype of officer whose behavior is severely problematic enough to warrant a label of prob-

---

2. I use the terms police misconduct, police deviance, and problem behaviors interchangeably throughout this work to note the same phenomenon.

lem officer. This research has theoretical and practical implications for both explaining and understanding these forms of problematic behavior, as well as how police executives might effectively control and manage them.

The Criminal Career Paradigm

There is an interesting analogy in criminology to the research on problem officers—a small percentage of criminals account for a disproportionate amount of the crime committed. Criminologists have labeled these offenders *career criminals* and devoted a great deal of time and effort in attempting to prospectively identify and incapacitate these offenders as a means of lowering the crime rate, with limited success. But criminologists went further. They developed a way of understanding the longitudinal sequence of offending for all criminals, which is commonly known as the criminal career paradigm.

This notion of examining a criminal's entire history of offending over time has had a significant impact on how the field thinks about the etiology, maintenance, and elimination of antisocial behavior, and has generated a wealth of information about the longitudinal patterning of criminal activity (for a review, see Piquero et al., 2003). It should be emphasized here however that the criminal career framework is not a theory of crime, but a way of structuring and organizing knowledge about certain key features of offending for observation and measurement (Blumstein et al., 1988). In short, it calls attention to certain key elements of an offender's career.

There are five key elements that characterize an offender's criminal career. The first, *onset*, is defined as the point at which an offender engages in his/her first criminal act. The next logical element within this framework is the notion of *desistance*, or the point at which an offender begins to disengage from criminal behavior. The third element, *duration*, is the length of time between onset and desistance. Included in the duration of a criminal's career there is the concept of *frequency*, or the total number of offenses by those criminally active in a given unit of time. The final concept is that of *participation*, which represents the proportion of those in a population who have ever engaged in crime. This concept serves to separate the offenders from the non-offenders in the population.

The prominence of characterizing criminal behavior in terms of a career framework largely began with the publications of Blumstein and his colleagues (Blumstein et al. 1986, 1988; Barnett et al. 1987, 1989, 1992). This set of research initially focused on the feasibility of predicting the future course of criminal careers, as Blumstein et al. (1986) argued that it was impossible to predict who will or will not be a high-rate offender, or understand the effects of criminal justice sanctioning on offenders' behavior more generally, without some body of knowledge about criminal careers.

While the work was intriguing, some criminologists called into question the entire criminal career approach, arguing that attempts to identify career criminals (or other offenders) would certainly fail. This critique, led by Gottfredson and Hirschi (1986), spurred much subsequent research on criminal careers which have raised important theoretical and methodological issues that are pertinent to adopting a developmental view of police misconduct. Such issues need to be understood before applying the criminal career paradigm to police deviance, and as such, are addressed in some detail below.

Controversy over the Criminal Career Paradigm

Despite its considerable impact on the field of criminology, the criminal career has not been accepted without controversy. The criminological literature includes a number of intense debates related to the criminal career, but for current purposes two are most relevant. The first debate focuses upon whether or not the relationship between past and future offending is a genuine causal link. The second involves how to best explain the stable relationship found between age and crime.

Some theories, such as Gottfredson and Hirschi's (1990) self-control theory, posit that criminal behavior is related to only one factor that can explain the entirety of criminal careers. For these theorists, the cause of crime is static and is represented by an enduring trait (e.g., self-control) that does not change with life circumstances. This theory, and others like them, is referred to as a *persistent heterogeneity* or *latent trait* explanation of crime (Nagin and Paternoster, 1991). In causal terms, these theories claim the positive correlation between past and future offending is spurious insofar as variation in both variables is the outcome of a common cause (Paternoster et al., 1997). If differences in criminal propensity between individuals—called *population heterogeneity*—are held constant, then the effects of life events of all sorts (including prior offending) should have no effect on subsequent offending. This point is key in that Gottfredson and Hirschi argue that offenders are different in degree and not kind; they do not allow for the existence of qualitatively different offender groups such as career criminals (Piquero et al., 2003). All criminal career elements are thus explained by a latent trait: as criminal propensity increases, so does frequency, duration, desistance, and overall participation in crime, while age of onset decreases.

The criminal career theorists instead argue that the underlying causes of crime are dynamic, and as such life circumstances can change one's capacity for criminal behavior. This explanation, commonly referred to as a *state-dependent* effect in the literature, posits that the effect of committing a crime reduces inhibitions and/or enhances the impetus to commit crime through a number of different mechanisms (e.g., loss of social capital, breaking of bonds to conventional society, etc.). As Nagin and Paternoster (2000) write, "The state dependence process, then, is a process of contagion in which an offender's current activities make their life circumstances worse, accelerating the probability of future crime" (p. 118). But there is a positive side to state dependence as well. Noncriminal behavior, such as steady employment or marrying a nondeviant spouse, can decrease the probability of offending. Just as criminal behavior can make things worse, conventional behavior can make one's life circumstances better. So, unlike persistent heterogeneity, state dependence allows for different predictors of the different criminal career elements, and also allows for qualitatively different groups of offenders.

Interestingly, research emerging from this theoretical debate has found support for both perspectives (for a review see Nagin and Paternoster, 2000). Based on a decade or so worth of research involving different data sets and different modeling strategies, there are no unequivocal conclusions to draw for either theoretical perspective. Persistent heterogeneity does seem to contribute in part to the observed continuity of offending over time, and people do differ with respect to their propensity to commit crime at a very early age (Nagin and Farrington 1992a, b; Paternoster et al., 1997). However, time-varying characteristics also matter. Despite the differences in criminal propensity early in life, individuals' life events or experiences can lead to both short-term and long-term change in criminal offending (Horney et al., 1995; Sampson and Laub, 1993).

Another challenge which highlights the difference between latent trait and state dependence theorists is how each explains one of the most stable relationships in criminology—the age-crime curve. There is a vast amount of evidence to suggest that generally, criminal involvement in the population rises from childhood through adolescence, generally peaks at about age 18, and then begins a steady decline thereafter (Farrington, 1986). An interesting challenge arises in explaining the age-crime curve when a theory claims that crime is the result of an enduring trait that does not change. Gottfredson and Hirschi argue (somewhat enigmatically) that the age-crime curve is a direct effect of aging unmitigated by other criminological constructs. In other words, the age-crime curve is invariant, persisting regardless of race, sex, country, time, or offense (Hirschi & Gottfredson, 1983).[3] Proponents of the criminal career

---

3. This assertion is not supported by available data. While most age-crime curves display similar features, measures of magnitude, central tendency, dispersion and skewness of the curves vary with time, place, sex, and crime type (Farrington, 1986).

perspective instead argue that the aggregate age-crime curve is comprised of increasing number of adolescents entering their criminal careers. This explains the rise in the age-crime curve during the early teenage years. Once the curve is peaked, fewer and fewer people start their criminal careers, and many of the current offenders desist, resulting in the sharp decrease in the age-crime curve. Those who remain criminals commit crimes at a steady rate, so the criminal career proponents argue that the age-crime curve is explained by participation (i.e., a change in number of active offenders in the population) and not frequency (i.e., the number of offenses committed by an active offender). To determine which of these two explanations is accurate in explaining the age-crime curve, one must know if this aggregate pattern is similar to, or different from, the pattern of individual offenders.

This key issue, whether the aggregate pattern of the age-crime curve holds at the individual level, was addressed by Nagin & Land (1993), and later replicated in Land et al. (1996). The authors employed an innovative statistical technique called the semiparametric, group-based approach, which takes into account both observed and unobserved heterogeneity in the offender population, and separates a finite number of offenders into "clumps." Each "clump" is internally homogeneous, but differs in the risk of offending from other "clumps." The model can estimate the probability that any given individual will fall into each "clump" found in the data. The "clump" to which one most likely belongs can be used as an indicator of unobserved criminal propensity (Nagin & Paternoster, 2000).

The authors discovered that in the Cambridge Study in Delinquent Development, individual offending was not age invariant as previously suggested by Blumstein and his colleagues, but instead was single peaked, much like the aggregate curve. While this supports Gottfredson and Hirschi's position, both camps neglect the idea that while individuals not only consistently differ in their rate of offending at different ages, they may also have distinctive paths of offending *over* age (Nagin & Land, 1993). In fact, the authors find that only some offenders follow the pattern of the aggregate age-crime curve, while others follow two distinctly different offending paths. One group began offending early, and continued at a high rate between the ages of 12 to 22 (about 1.0–1.2 convictions per year), which then began to drop off and decline to about .35 by age 30. The other group, which had the flattest age-crime curve, had the lowest rate of offending, but persisted at this low rate throughout the sampling period. This study demonstrates that with regard to the age-crime curve, both Gottfredson and Hirschi's and Blumstein's and his colleagues' hypotheses were incomplete. At the individual level, some individuals follow the aggregate age-crime curve, but some do not. Some individuals follow an offending path much different from the aggregate curve.

Similar results were found in Land et al. (1996). Using the Philadelphia Second Cohort data and the same semiparametric, group-based approach, the authors found that individual offending was single-peaked, similar to the findings in the Cambridge data. In addition, the authors found evidence of the same three offender pathways discovered by Nagin and Land (1993), providing more evidence that at the individual level, not all offenders follow the aggregate age-crime curve.

The conclusions derived from this body of research are enormously important in that they emphasize the non-exclusive nature of the state dependent and latent trait perspectives. The two explanations of criminal behavior do not need to be regarded as mutually exclusive, and in fact both may be required in an adequate explanation of a person's career offending pattern. While there appear to be enduring, time-stable characteristics that explain offending, they alone are not as powerful an explanation of crime as models that include periods of active offending and periods of quiescence. Moreover, the age-crime curve need not only consist of an offending pattern that follows the aggregate curve or consist of offenders who have a steady frequency, but instead may consist of differing offending patterns by age and over time. The challenge to criminologists now is to offer meaningful theoretical explanations of crime that account for these empirical findings.

Life-Course Theory and Developmental Criminology

Enter the life-course theorists. The life-course perspective views people's life-course trajectories as a sequence of causal factors in which dependent variables become independent variables over time (Elder, 1985). The life course here is defined as "pathways through the age differentiated life span" (Elder, 1985). Two concepts are central to life-course theory: a trajectory and a transition. A *trajectory* is a pathway of development over the life span, such as work, parenthood, or criminal behavior. A *transition* is marked by life events (e.g., first job, first child born, first crime) that are embedded in trajectories and evolve over shorter time spans (Sampson & Laub, 1993).

This life-course paradigm is concerned with explaining stability as well as discontinuity in behaviors over the life course. Therefore, this perspective focuses upon life events (such as crimes) and age-graded transitions (i.e., transitions into adult roles) that either change or strengthen current behavior. This framework is advantageous in that it leads one away from concentrating on restricted periods in the life cycle (e.g., during adolescence) or restricted groupings of persons (e.g., career criminals) (Hagan & Palloni, 1988). A developmental or life-course explanation can include differing explanations of the elements of a criminal career, and can also include different offender types based on these explanations. Additionally, such explanations do not focus on the immediate precursors or consequences of criminal behavior. While most crime is committed during the teenage years, developmental theorists look for roots marked by earlier behaviors that do not begin in adolescence, but childhood (Thornberry, 1997). Likewise, these theorists also recognize that criminal involvement has consequences for a person's subsequent development, and encourage thinking about the ways in which crime can influence the success and timing of life-graded transitions. Thus, the criminal career paradigm fostered growth in developmental criminology as a way to apply concepts of human development to explaining criminal careers.

The life-course perspective offers a view of crime that is different from both the state-dependent and the latent trait explanations of crime. Both the latent trait and state-dependent explanations seem to offer a common explanation of crime that applies to all members of the population. The latent trait perspective offers the suggestion that all crimes can be attributed to self-control or some other enduring personality trait. The state-dependent perspective instead argues that the commission of a criminal act reduces future inhibitions and/or strengthens the motivations to commit crime (Paternoster et al., 1997). The life-course perspective, conversely, suggests multiple pathways to crime, which, in part, is due to the research on criminal careers that suggested the existence of different offender types. This work, while good at identifying offender types, was often criticized for not providing adequate explanations for these career types (Tittle, 1988). The resurgence in this literature began when the life-course theorists rejected the assumption of a common theoretical explanation for all offending patterns, and suggested instead that different offender types may require different causal explanations unique to that offender type.

A number of examples could be cited as cases of developmental theories, and in fact many existing criminological theories are compatible with the developmental perspective (see, for example, Thornberry, 1997). However, two cases will be illustrative here. One, a taxonomy developed by Moffitt (1993), shows how both state-dependent and persistent heterogeneity explanations can be utilized to explain criminal behavior and the age-crime curve. The other, by Sampson and Laub (1993), demonstrates how consideration of the degree of successful adaptation to age-graded social transitions can either help or hinder one's capacity to commit crime, thereby changing one's trajectory of criminal behavior throughout the life course. These examples are covered in detail because they will be alluded to in subsequent chapters.

Moffitt (1993) argues that the overall delinquent population contains two distinct types of offenders. The first distinct type, who she labels *life-course persistent* (LCP) offenders, begin exhibiting antisocial behavior early and maintain a high rate of antisocial behavior over the life course. According to her theory, LCP offenders' problem behaviors start early and persist because neurodevelopmental impairments lead to deficient self-control, which disrupts normal socialization and makes these individuals particularly vulnerable to criminogenic social environments. The second type, labeled *adolescence-limited* (AL), begins antisocial behavior much later in life, and this behavior is temporary, situational, and according to Moffitt, normative. More specifically, these youth lack any personal propensity to commit crime, but they nevertheless become time-limited delinquents in an effort to break free from childhood constraints by mimicking deviant peers during their adolescent years (Jeglum-Bartusch et al., 1997). For Moffitt, the low levels of crime seen in late childhood and throughout adulthood in the age-crime curve are actually the same people who have been offending all their lives, while the peak in the age-crime curve represents a large number of adolescents who join with these early and life-long offenders in committing crime, but desist from offending in adulthood.

One can see from her explanation that Moffitt shares a similar idea of the role of criminal propensity that was advocated by Gottfredson and Hirschi. However, Moffitt's developmental theory diverges from Gottfredson and Hirschi's work by arguing that age will influence the strength of correlations between measures of propensity and criminal participation. Because the LCP offenders account for the vast number of offenders in early childhood and late adulthood, measures of criminal propensity should correlate strongly during these life periods. However, during adolescence, the LCP offenders are vastly outnumbered by the AL offenders, who lack a strong criminal propensity, so the measures should correlate weakly at this age period.

Sampson and Laub (1993) posit a different developmental theory, but like Moffitt's, it can incorporate both stability and change in criminal behavior. Sampson and Laub begin with the central premise of social control theory—that crime and deviance are more likely when an individual's bond to society is weak or broken—as an organizing principle for their theory which emphasizes the social bonding over the life course (Sampson & Laub, 1993). The authors break down an individual's life-course in terms of age and state that the relative importance of formal and informal social institutions varies across the life span. The authors explain continuity of criminal behavior from childhood to adulthood by describing a developmental process whereby delinquent behavior attenuates the social and institutional bonds linking adults to society (e.g., labor force attachment, martial cohesion). However, not all antisocial children become antisocial adults, so the authors account for change or variation in adult crime by postulating that it is directly related to the strength of adult social bonds. How adults adapt to changing social roles and life events is crucial to Sampson and Laub. Despite connections between childhood events and adult experiences, turning points in the life course can redirect life paths. This also can explain why some individuals experience abrupt and radical "turnarounds" in their lives, providing a mechanism of late onset or sudden desistance of criminal behavior.

These two examples demonstrate how developmental or life-course theories have incorporated both state dependent and latent trait effects into a comprehensive framework that views criminal behavior as an event within a larger life trajectory. All people who commit crime or engage in antisocial behavior more generally do not necessarily have the same antecedents or follow the same patterns over time, which explains why some individuals have relatively short criminal careers, while others may offend early and continue to do so throughout their lives. This advancement in criminological theory has spurred new interest in research concerning criminal careers, and has been vital in outlining future research objectives for others to follow.

The Risk Factor Prevention Paradigm

The research on criminal careers and developmental criminology also helped narrow the gap between researchers interested in explaining crime and policy makers interested in preventing it. Research on criminal careers provided information about the onset, frequency, persistence, and desistance of offending, and consistently found a small number of offenders who contributed disproportionately to the total number of offenses. This led policy makers to be concerned about identifying these frequent offenders in advance and devising programs to prevent their delinquent development.

This concern gave rise to what Farrington (2000) calls the *risk factor prevention paradigm*, which is premised on the simple idea of, "identifying the key risk factors for offending and implement prevention methods designed to counteract them. There is often a related attempt to identify key protective factors against offending and to implement prevention methods designed to enhance them" (p. 1). A *risk factor* is a characteristic or variable that predicts an increased probability of later offending. This term can refer to an extreme category on an explanatory variable (e.g., poor parental supervision) or a dichotomous variable contrasting the presence or absence of some characteristic (e.g., being male). These have a different meaning in the literature than a correlate or later outcome. A *correlate* usually refers to factors that occur at the same time as the outcome and that statistically covaries with it (Loeber, 1990). *Protective factors*, conversely, are those factors that mediate or moderate the effect of exposure to risk factors, resulting in reduced incidence of problem behavior (Pollard et al., 1999).

While the risk factor prevention paradigm has been increasing in influence in criminology, it does have weaknesses. A key advantage of this paradigm is that it is easy to communicate and links explanation and prevention. Risk factors are based on empirical research rather than on theories, avoiding difficult theoretical questions about the mechanisms underlying the effects of risk factors on antisocial behavior. The large disadvantage of this paradigm, however, is that it encounters problems determining which risk factors are causes and which are merely correlated with causes (Farrington, 2000). Risk factors tend to co-occur, making them difficult to disentangle in terms of establishing developmental processes, and in terms of modeling these effects statistically. This is further complicated by the idea that certain risk factors may vary by criminal career element (e.g., onset, frequency, etc.) and may be different for different people (e.g., males versus females) (Farrington, 2000). Ideally, one would want to target only risk factors that are causes, as interventions targeting merely markers of causes would have no (or little) effect.

Enhancing Our Understanding of Police Misconduct

Theoretical Lessons

Having discussed criminal careers specifically and developmental criminology more generally, one might ask: what can these frameworks tell researchers about police misconduct? After all, the police are the crime-fighters, not the crime-committers, right? The police certainly engage in a number of activities, some legal (e.g., discourtesy), and some illegal (e.g., stealing from a crime scene) under a broad definition of misconduct. In this respect, police misconduct, much like crime, can be considered under the general concept of antisocial behavior, which is the focus of developmental criminology. Indeed, developmental criminology considers a whole host of acts under the rubric of antisocial behavior, many of which are not crimes per se, either because the subject under consideration is incapable of crime (e.g., the subject is a juvenile), or the behavior is only crime-related (e.g., a psychological disorder). Moreover, what is and is not a legal act changes over time and across varying locations, so it makes sense to not study criminal behavior specifically, but antisocial behaviors more generally. The difference is that crimes are violations of law, while antisocial behaviors are common transgressions against societal norms. When the latter term is used, different expressions over the life-course can be more easily taken into account. To say that antisocial behavior is continued does not necessarily imply a specific behavior is continued from childhood to adulthood, but rather that across the life-course, individuals manifest antisocial behaviors that may change across time and in different situations. Police misconduct certainly can be conceived of as a violation of societal norms, and thus can be considered under a developmental framework.

But research on police misconduct, and police research in general, does little to consider the causes and consequences of behavior over the course of an officer's career. By stressing the examination of misconduct over time, researchers can begin to advance their thinking of police misconduct along the same lines as developmental criminology. This can start by thinking in career terms and considering in the aggregate the five criminal career elements of onset, desistance, duration, frequency, and participation, as well as examining the different trajectories of problem behaviors at the individual level.

It should be stressed, however, that *borrowing concepts from the criminal career literature does not necessarily imply that criminals and police officers have the same underlying causes of antisocial behavior.* Recall earlier that the criminal career paradigm is not a theory of crime, and in fact has been criticized for being atheoretical. This paradigm simply provides one with tools for examining antisocial behavior over time; it does not provide one with explanation for those observed behaviors. Thus, the primary purpose of the research presented here is exploratory in that it seeks to determine if distinct patterns of police misconduct exist over time. The data described later in Chapter 3 do not adequately provide variables that would explain the patterns that one might observe, although the data do contain characteristics that may be deemed risk factors, protective factors, and correlates. The important first step is to determine what kinds of patterns exist that are worth explaining.

Developmental criminology does provide explanations of antisocial behavior with the concepts of persistent heterogeneity, state dependence, and additional consideration of how the two might compliment each other to increase explanatory power. Persistent heterogeneity implies an enduring trait that does not change, but simply differs in degree between individuals, and therefore might be seen as a way of explaining similarly the antisocial behavior of both criminals and police officers (or the entire population who engage in antisocial behavior more generally). The difference between the two groups is simply the amount of criminal potential in each individual.

One might initially theorize that criminals would possess much less self-control than police officers, especially given that highly antisocial people would have neither the inclination to endure the lengthy process of becoming a police officer, nor meet the background or educational requirements to even apply for the position. But the police themselves most likely screen out only the most extreme antisocial applicants. Psychological testing of potential applicants leaves much to be desired, and few, if any, have been rigorously validated (Grant & Grant, 1996). Moreover, many police departments are under tremendous pressure to diversify their occupation and hire female and minority candidates. This may sometimes leave police to recruit from a limited pool of candidates that meet affirmative action requirements, some of which, if the candidates were white or male, would not have been hired. So, it is at least plausible that while the most antisocial individuals would not find their way into modern police agencies, those who may possess more antisocial tendencies than the average individual may still find a way inside. This is not unique to the police world, and is probably true of most other occupations. This also does not mean these applicants last long in a police agency either.

State dependence, on the other hand, provides a different explanation of antisocial behavior, and may not operate for police and criminals in the same manner. This concept claims that life circumstances makes a difference in the likelihood of engaging in antisocial behavior, and directs one to structural characteristics of the offender's environment. Here one can think of a myriad of differences between the criminal and the police officer. The police have a certain number of unique occupational characteristics, such as the capacity to use coercion, the low-visibility of the work, etc, which may contribute to a change in a given individual's probability of engaging in deviance. So, for example, even if a new recruit has few antisocial tendencies, these may be made manifest by a department which allows officers to engage in graft. Alternatively, a person with an above average propensity to engage in deviance might be suppressed if they were to join a police force in which officers are effectively mentored and closely supervised. This is not to say that certain life events will not operate similarly for criminals and police officers, as one might expect that getting married or having children would be a significant life event that would mitigate against future deviance for either group.

Taking this notion further it can be argued, as developmental criminologists do, that one explanation may not be adequate for all offending patterns, requiring different causal explanation unique to different sets of offenders. As such, there may be different causal mechanisms at work for police misconduct patterns just as there may be different causal mechanisms at work for criminal offending patterns. For example, some officers might be "adolescent-limited" in their misconduct, being likely to engage in problematic behaviors early in their career until they mature and become skilled in police work. Other officers may be "life-course persistent" in their misconduct, being likely to engage in misconduct across their career course. Across these two groups, the mechanisms explaining police deviance could be similar or extremely divergent.

Additionally, the risk factor prevention paradigm has something to say about exploring risk and protective factors, and how they can be utilized in interventions. EI systems already attempt to scan behaviors thought to indicate "at-risk" behaviors, but police interventions can go further by considering what occupational hazards exist that may be risk factors for misconduct, and also consider what protective factors exist that might mitigate against deviance. The goal of course would be to lessen risk factors while enhancing protective factors as a means of lowering the overall incidence of problem behaviors.

Methodological Lessons

Besides the theoretical concepts the criminal career paradigm and developmental criminology can bring to bear on police misconduct, there are a number of methodological lessons to be learned as well. Indeed, early criminal career research relied almost exclusively on official data as a measure of deviance (in terms of arrests or convictions for serious crimes), and so does research on police misconduct (in terms of citizen complaints, civil litigation, uses of force, etc.). As such, many of the same shortcomings related to the use of official data in criminal career research apply to the use of official data in understanding police misconduct.

Criminal career researchers have noted the disadvantages of official data in terms of its undercounting the number of actual offenses, its unreliable recording, and the difficulty in deciding between measuring crime by arrests or convictions. Also, criminal career researchers noted the need to control for exposure time in estimations of criminal career dimensions, offender heterogeneity, and the problem of false onset and desistance. Many of these problems hold for research on police misconduct as well.

Take for instance the fact that official data represents only a small amount of an offender's actual offending. Criminologists know from comparisons with self-report data that arrests or convictions only account for a fraction of a given offender's actual criminal behavior over the course of a specified period. The same could be said for police misconduct. Relying on official data such as citizen complaints has a number of drawbacks, one of which is that they represent only a small percentage of an officer's actual misconduct. Police scholars know from survey research that not every citizen who is treated poorly by the police complains, or is successful if he/she makes an attempt to complain.

Blumstein et al. (1985) developed an estimation procedure to infer the number of criminal acts committed by an offender from their arrest records. Assuming that an individual's crime rate (λ) is independent of the probability for arrest for a crime (q), the individual arrest rate (μ) is the product of the individual crime rate and the risk of arrest per crime: $\mu = \lambda q$. Of course, some estimate of arrest for a crime is needed. To do this, Blumstein et al. estimated the risk of arrest from aggregate data. Assuming all offenders face the same arrest risk, one can estimate a ratio of the number of reported arrests for an offense type (A) and divide by the number of reported crimes (C). The number of reported crimes must be adjusted for the fact that only a fraction of crimes are actually reported to the police (r). Additionally, since many crimes are committed in groups, the number of arrests must be divided by the average number of offenders per criminal events, (O). The final estimate per crime of type i is:

$$q_i = \frac{A_i / O_i}{C_i / r_i}$$

A similar estimation might be made for the number of misconduct-related offenses in which an officer engages from the number of complaints they receive. Of course, one would have to devise a strategy to estimate the probability of a complaint (q). Walker and Bumphus (1992, p. 11), in a review of studies that examined citizen reporting of police misconduct, noted that there was a "striking similarity" between the frequency to which citizens report crimes to the police, and the frequency to which citizens report police misconduct, leading the authors to conclude, "It is reasonable ... that official complaints received by police departments represent about one-third of all incidents of alleged police misconduct."[4]

Another concern with using official data is the degree to which it is unreliably recorded. Data that must be recorded in electronic form is subject to entry error, and this is true of not just aggregate crime measures such as the UCR. Records kept by police agencies

---

4. Such a conclusion was drawn primarily from the Police Services Study, which employed a victimization survey and found that out of the 13.6 percent of citizens who felt mistreated by the police in the previous year, only about 30 percent filed a formal complaint (Whitaker, 1982).

on their employees are also subject to such error. This is an especially valid concern when multiple indicators of police misconduct must be obtained from various departments within a police agency. In large agencies in particular, data may be located in different places: citizen complaints may be kept in the internal affairs bureau, while information on civil suits may be maintained by the legal department, and information regarding sick leave may be held in the accounting office. Each department may be better or worse at maintaining their respective data, creating different sets of data with varying degrees of reliability. Pulling these different sources of data together into a form that can be readily analyzed adds another step that increases opportunity for error.

There is also the problem of deciding between arrests or convictions. Arrests might include false arrests, so one might favor using convictions, but the factors associated with whether one receives a disposition after any particular arrest is often not associated with factual guilt or innocence, so a choice between the two must be carefully weighed. There is a similar problem with using citizen complaints against the police. Using citizen complaints as a measure of police misconduct brings with them the existence of false complaints. That is, a citizen may bring a complaint against an officer when he/she is not guilty of misconduct, either because the citizen does not understand police procedure, or to gain legal advantage on the officer (e.g., in the case of an arrest). To avoid this type of error, one might use citizen complaints that were investigated and found to have merit. In this case, one has more confidence that the officer is actually guilty of whatever misconduct the citizen has claimed. However, such a strategy is limiting as previous research demonstrates that in the vast majority of cases, the only person witnessing an alleged act of misconduct is the complainant. Such cases become "swearing contests" in which the officer and citizen allege their version of events is true, with these cases resulting in a complaint being unsubstantiated (i.e., there is no way to prove or disprove the allegation). In most research utilizing official data, criminal career researchers have often used arrests, noting that the incidence of false arrests are small, especially when compared to errors of commission that would occur if only convictions were used. In research on police misconduct, most examinations utilizing citizen complaints examine all complaints (or a subset thereof) filed against an officer, regardless of disposition.

Criminal career researchers have also noted the problem of controlling for time at risk, referring to time when an offender is "off the street" (i.e., incarcerated, in the hospital for a prolonged period of time, etc.), when estimating criminal career dimensions. There is a similar problem for examining police misconduct. First, police officers, like in many other occupations, may be out on sick leave or disability, and hence off the street and not vulnerable to citizen complaints. Second, police officers might receive disciplinary action for a number of activities while on the job, and this can include suspension for a period of time. This also excludes the officer from opportunities to engage in misconduct. Third, there is the need to consider the officer's rank. Patrol officers have much more contact with the public than sergeants, lieutenants, captains, and the upper echelon of a police hierarchy. Therefore, officers who have a rank above that of a patrol officer are at a decreased risk of receiving a citizen complaint because of a decreased amount of exposure time to the general public. Fourth, it is important to consider the activity of an officer's beat or assignment. All patrol officers have a great deal of exposure to citizens, but some areas of a city may have a higher level of this exposure compared to others. For example, a beat that is located in a high-crime area, or an area that receives a large number of calls for police service, certainly places officers in that beat at a higher risk for citizen complaints than a relatively placid area with very little crime or calls for service.

Any estimation of an officer's frequency of misconduct must include a control for the officer's time at risk. Such a control would take into account the officer's rank, characteristics of their beat or assignment, and would also note prolonged periods of absence from street duty, such as a long stretch of sick leave days or a suspension from duty. Failure to do so will cause misestimations in misconduct dimensions such as frequency and duration.

Population heterogeneity is less a concern in police research, since no study has yet to look at misconduct over officer's careers. It is a problem, however, in police research which examines citizen complaints over brief time periods. Since officers who are most problematic are presumably the ones most likely to generate citizen complaints, any study examining these complaints for any one year (or any relatively short time period) will over-represent these types of officers, and moreover, will not be able to account for officers who have yet to begin their misconduct or who have desisted, both of which are placed into a "non-problem" category.

There is also the problem of false onset and desistance. There is difficulty in observing offenders for a duration long enough to be certain they have stopped offending. People may cease offending and then restart after some prolonged time period (possibly years), perhaps because of negative turning points in the life course (e.g. the start of drug use, separation from a spouse, loss of employment, etc.). Also when using official data, the age of adult responsibility is 18, and without access to juvenile records, it is difficult to determine if an offender began his/her criminal activity prior to that age. Estimating age of onset becomes difficult under these circumstances, and some research has simply assumed onset before age 18 or ignored the first arrest of sample members in late adolescence (ages 18–20) in estimations of frequency (Blumstein and Cohen, 1979).

There is an additional problem when using official data in estimating desistance since some criminals might become more adept at avoiding detection over time. In this case, a criminal's offending does not change, but as they become better criminals, the frequency with which they are arrested might decrease over time, leading to the assumption of a desistance processes when in fact none exists. It is simply that the offender has become more adept at avoiding detection from the criminal justice system.

Similar problems exist for research on police misconduct. Fortunately, researchers do not have to wait until police officers reach a certain age before one can begin to gather official data on their behavior; such data can be collected at the start of the officer's career. Thus, for each officer one has a clear point at which data collection can begin. One also has a clear stopping point—the date the officer retires or leaves the police force.[5] However, while false onset is less of a problem in police misconduct, there still exists the false desistance problem. Police researchers often suppose that officers generally decrease in their frequency of problem behaviors with experience as a result of maturation (both personal and professional). But this may also suggest that officers get better at avoiding detection of their problem behaviors, or become more adept at avoiding situations where citizens may be apt to complain, thereby decreasing the number of official complaints on their record, even if their problem behavior has not been corrected.

Research on criminal careers has faced a number of methodological challenges with the use of official data, and while these challenges are not insurmountable, any criminological research using these data must indeed be cognizant of their inherent drawbacks. Using official data to examine police misconduct over time will invariably suffer from similar drawbacks. Problems of the unrepresentativeness of official data, its unreliability in recording and selectivity presents problems for any research. The additional problems of controlling for exposure time and accounting for false desistance present challenges as well.

Conclusion

It is important to understand how developments in criminology, moving from a focus on career criminals to an understanding of these offenders within a larger framework of criminal careers, have been shaped by progress both theoretically and methodologically since its emergence in the early 1980s. Early work on criminal careers brought forth empirical questions about whether the

---

5. A problem arises, however, if an officer is transferred in from, or out to, another police agency.

causes of criminal behavior were static (i.e., a latent trait) or dynamic (i.e., state dependent) and the function of the aggregate age-crime curve at the individual level.

From the discussion of these issues, it is apparent that the debate between the latent trait and the state dependent theorists has resulted in a realization that the two explanations are not mutually exclusive, and in fact both are required to understand criminal behavior. Moreover, while the criminal career model has suggested distinct types of criminals, the life-course theorists, who see crime in terms of larger life-course trajectories, have expanded upon this early model. From this work, distinct criminal career trajectories have emerged, and criminologists have been challenged to develop explanations for these offender types.

Theory about police misconduct certainly has not advanced this far. Indeed, while research of both criminal careers and police misconduct started with the common interest of predicting and explaining high-rate "offenders" (career criminals and problem officers, respectively) prompted by the promise of directing early interventions for these groups, police research has yet to progress to a stage which considers problem officers within a larger framework of police careers. Moreover, some of the work on police misconduct assumes an underlying predisposition towards deviance, much in the same vein as the latent trait theorists assumed criminal behavior was the result of an underlying predisposition that was enduring. Very few explanations of police behavior consider more proximal explanations or state dependent effects, and certainly there has been no attempt to integrate the two into a comprehensive framework of police misconduct. In addition, while there has been work on distinct police typologies, no one has considered whether there might be distinct individual career trajectories of police misconduct. Could there be a relationship between experience and misconduct that is meaningful and stable, similar to the age-crime curve? If it does exist, might there be distinct trajectories of police misconduct which underlie this curve? Such interesting questions can only be answered by taking a developmental view of police misconduct.

Chapter 2

Towards a Developmental View of Police Misconduct

"A policeman who becomes a thief does so for the same reasons that others are thieves—inclination and opportunity."

— Jonathan Rubenstein, *City Police*

The above quote by Rubenstein sums up nicely a *persistent heterogeneity* view of police misconduct. Such a view would explain police misconduct as tied to some criminal propensity or inclination that is differentially distributed across police personnel, which accounts for between-individual variations in antisocial acts. Of course, police officers are not a random sample, so such criminal propensity would not be normally distributed across the police population; if anything, such a distribution would be right censored, with the majority of cases located at the low end of criminal propensity, given that police screen applicants and have minimum standards for entry. Opportunity also plays a role, and serves to explain within-individual variation in police misconduct over time.

Other views of police misconduct can be considered *state dependent* in nature. Such views would see future acts of misconduct as enhanced by commission of present acts, which in turn reduces inhibitions and/or strengthens motivations for deviance. The slippery slope argument that explains the progressively increasing seriousness of police corruption is a state dependent view of misconduct. As officers become more comfortable with free meals, discounts on gifts, and the like, the argument goes, they become more willing to take increasingly-questionable payoffs: letting bars stay open later for free drinks, accepting bribes from motorists, etc. (Sherman, 1974). A similar view could also be posed for improper force. Officers may engage in improper force early in their career as a means of controlling situations, largely because they have yet to learn the art of persuasion and therefore tend to rely on their coercive authority, and, once successful and unpunished for such acts, may continue to do so in a wider array of citizen contacts (Chevigny, 1990).

Yet other state dependent effects may help temper the likelihood of misconduct, such as strict monitoring by front-line supervisors, or factors that are not job-related, such as marrying a nondeviant spouse, having children, etc. The number and nature of factors that could increase or decrease the likelihood of misconduct can come from both the research on police misconduct and from research on antisocial behavior more generally.

Of course, both state dependence and persistent heterogeneity can be complimentary explanations if brought under a developmental view. Such dynamic explanations of antisocial behavior which consider the interplay of persistent antisocial traits and state dependent effects over time hold many advantages over static theories of crime, and have added much to our ability to investigate the etiology and consequences of antisocial behavior. In a similar vein, dynamic explanations of police misconduct could also enhance our examinations of this behavior. A police officer's involvement in misconduct can be conceived as a developmental trajectory, which is possible given it has a distinct beginning and end. As such, this involvement can be described using misconduct "career" elements (adopting the five criminal career elements) of onset, duration, frequency, desistance, and participation. This line of inquiry can go even further by considering the life-course view that distinct pathways may underlie an aggregate career-course.[1] Such a discourse, if it is to begin, would first focus on the relationship between misconduct and experience as a police officer, attempt to

---

1. The notion that police misconduct can be seen as a part of larger life-course trajectory in antisocial behavior, such that the start of a police ca-

identify distinct patterns of such behavior, and then examine possible correlates of these patterns.

Before considering police misconduct from a developmental perspective, the dependent variable needs to be clarified and more closely examined. Indeed, police misconduct is a rather vague term and therefore means different things to different people. Also, to be able to consider this behavior over time, this work will tend to focus on some forms of police misconduct while neglecting others. Specifically, this work focuses on less serious forms of misconduct characterized as problematic police behaviors.

Defining Police Misconduct

Police misconduct, sometimes also referred to as police deviance or improper police behavior in the literature, is a broad term encompassing a vast array of antisocial behaviors, and indeed police scholars have made several attempts to categorize these acts. Some have made a distinction between acts of misconduct which are facilitated by the officer's position, and thus can only be committed by police, and those that are not (Kappeler et al., 1984). Acts facilitated by the position include police corruption, such as accepting bribes or stealing from a crime scene, or abuses of authority, such as using secondary arrest charges as a means of covering up a use of improper force, or engaging in illegal searches and seizures of citizens. These acts of misconduct are distinct amongst police as they stem from the authority granted by their occupation, and are different from other crimes which police officers can commit and are not facilitated by the position (e.g., domestic violence). The latter are simply the same acts in which the public engages.

But crimes committed by the police are not the only acts which should be considered under a definition of police misconduct. The

---

reer is a turning point that either increases or decreases antisocial behavior, is also an interesting one, but is beyond the scope of this book.

penal code is generally vague, and does not provide an adequate guide to police for what is and is not acceptable behavior (Fyfe et al., 1997). Even some acts of excessive force on the part of police do not fall under the penal code of simple or aggravated assault. There are many other acts of deviance in which the police can engage as well, which are occupationally located, that are not criminal but discouraged by the edicts of police professionalism. Such acts include being rude or verbally abusive to citizens, sleeping on the job, driving recklessly, etc. These forms of misconduct can be relatively minor when compared to fully criminal acts committed by police, but are nevertheless important to consider under the full spectrum of misconduct.

Since a developmental perspective of police misconduct would want to examine all the different forms of misconduct across officer careers, a broad definition of misconduct is preferred. Such a definition must encompass acts which are criminal and noncriminal, as well as acts facilitated by the position or not. The true distinguishing characteristic of police misconduct, and the one which sets it apart from other forms of deviance, is that it is an antisocial act committed by someone who is a police officer. This definition is simple, but it allows one to take different manifestations of police misconduct across career spans into account.

The different types of misconduct noted above, while valuable in illustrating the full range of police deviance, also illustrate several challenges for adopting a developmental view of police misconduct. First, some misconduct is very serious, so much so that it will be an extremely rare occurrence, and will also likely lead to career termination when discovered.[2] Serious criminal acts on the part of the police (e.g., homicide, extortion, burglary) certainly fit this criterion and therefore could truncate or limit an officer's career trajectory. Relatedly, since presumably very serious acts of misconduct are a rare occurrence, it can be difficult to relate these behaviors in career

---

2. This is not to say that some kinds of serious misconduct go unpunished, as there are a myriad of examples, especially in the literature on corruption, of officers not being disciplined for such acts.

terms. If an officer engages in only one or two acts of misconduct, his/her career cannot effectively be characterized in career terms.

Second, misconduct is very difficult to measure empirically. Since officers have an incentive to cover or hide their antisocial behaviors, detecting them is an issue. No research has yet to ask officers to self-report on their own misconduct, presuming that officers would be uncooperative, so investigators have had to rely on citizen reporting of misconduct (via surveys or complaints filed with an agency), officers reporting of misconduct they have witnessed in their agency (via surveys or complaints made to supervisors), or the reports of observers conducting investigations of police work and who witness misconduct. Each one of these methods have strengths and weaknesses, but all will tend to note less serious forms of misconduct (e.g., discourtesy to citizens) since they occur with more frequency and are likely to be complained about. Other and more serious forms of misconduct, such as corruption, are difficult to detect, since both the officer engaged in corruption and citizens involved in such acts have an incentive not to reveal their behavior (Kutnjak Ivkovic, 2005). Thus, researchers interested in this issue have had to rely on case studies where corruption was detected and subsequently investigated (Sherman, 1978).

A developmental view of police misconduct, then, will tend to focus on less serious forms of misconduct—those not likely to end in career termination and occur with some frequency—so that these behaviors can be detected over time and characterized using the criminal career terms of onset, frequency, duration, desistance, and participation. This does not necessarily mean that theoretically a developmental view of misconduct cannot apply to career-ending misconduct, just that empirically, measuring police misconduct over time will tend to focus on somewhat less serious behaviors such as abuses of police authority.

Still, focusing on these somewhat less serious types of misconduct is important and can contribute to understanding and preventing deviance. Police administrators are certainly concerned with officers who commit very serious acts of misconduct, but the remedy is typically removal of such "rotten apples" from the force.

What are more likely to be of concern are the less serious, but more frequent, forms of misconduct which are amenable to intervention and have been the focus of new accountability mechanisms such as EIS. In addition, these are the types of behaviors that are of concern to citizens, since such behaviors are likely to cause friction between police and citizens in their day-to-day interactions. Research on citizen complaints bears this out: citizens typically complain about officers behaving in a rude or unprofessional manner, using unnecessary or excessive force, or neglecting their duties (Lersch, 1998; Lersch and Mieczkowski, 1996). Given that negative experiences appear to have a considerable impact on citizens' overall satisfaction with the police, which in turn may impact the degree to which citizens cooperate and provide information to the police, such less serious forms of police misconduct are important and not to be discounted (Bayley, 2002).

As such, police misconduct, as it is referred to herein, will tend to focus upon certain forms of misconduct such as occupationally-located deviance and abuses of police authority, while neglecting crimes committed by the police or acts of corruption. Specifically, these behaviors are of the types that occur with some frequency, citizens most complain about, and therefore routinely come under administrative inquiry. These types of behaviors, which are commonly termed *problem behaviors* or *problematic police performance* to reflect their less serious nature, more narrowly captures those behaviors that are the focus of this research. Other forms of police misconduct, such as serious criminal acts like robbery or homicide, are not investigated here. Again, this is largely due to the low frequency of such acts, the difficulty in uncovering them, and their likelihood of leading to career termination once discovered. Still, from a theoretical perspective, a developmental view of police misconduct can account for these behaviors, even if there is considerable difficulty in investigating them empirically.

A final component of defining police misconduct is specifying the unit of analysis. Thus far, viewing individual officers and their patterns of misconduct as developmental trajectories have been the focus of discussion. This is done to parallel the criminal career and developmental criminology literature, which focuses on individual offenders and their behavior over time. But, as an important side note, other theories could be posed which account for the career trajectories of groups of officers, such as those with the same assignment or who serve in the same specialized unit. Such a consideration would have the advantage of considering peer influences on deviance, noting that misconduct can occur as a group with cooperation from others. Other theories could be posed examining an entire agency's trajectory in misconduct, as Sherman (1978) notes that entire police agencies can be corrupt. Others have suggested that entire agencies can be brutal, and encourage unnecessary or excessive violence against citizens (Skolnick and Fyfe, 1993). Thus, agencies themselves can have an organizational trajectory in misconduct. Going beyond an individual-level explanation of misconduct over time is beyond the scope of this work, but it certainly could be undertaken.

How Experience Shapes Misconduct

Before considering how one might apply a career perspective to police deviance, it is important to consider how the process of becoming a police officer and "learning the ropes" can contribute to problem behaviors. While the work on police careers is sparse, there are some important findings to consider, and the work on other topics such as police productivity, the use of force on the part of police, and other forms of coercion and the like must also be considered. Moreover, cross-sectional police research also include measurements such as years of experience on the job, which can aid in the construction of a developmental framework, as well as provide empirical evidence regarding police behavior patterns over time.

The earliest research in the police literature that considers officer careers is the work on police socialization. Some of the earliest writings on police documented the existence of an occupationally located police "working personality," a set of unique attitudes and norms that differentiate the police and the public (Skolnick, 1975).

Specifically, there were two hypotheses as to how this "personality" emerged. Some maintained that police officers are significantly different *prior* to their entry into the occupation. This hypothesis argues that certain types of people seek out careers in law enforcement, where their authoritarian traits are accepted and even rewarded.[3] Another hypothesis maintains that the police "working personality" emerges because of the unique demands of the occupation, such as the constant threat of danger and the coercive authority granted to all police officers. This socialization hypothesis focuses on both the structure of the occupation and the process by which recruits eventually become experienced officers with a police "personality." This latter hypothesis is more congruent with a developmental view of police behavior and examines how an officer changes over time.

The body of socialization research covers many areas: the reasons for choosing the police as a profession, the recruits' experiences in the police academy and training, and their experiences with the first few days, weeks, months, and the first year or two on the job. Each piece suggests that there are numerous structural factors to confront, and these factors shape the processes by which a police recruit learns to become a police officer. Unfortunately, no one study covers officer misconduct extensively, but the research does make suggestions about what problem behaviors officers are likely to engage early in their career and why. Almost equally unfortunate is that no study considers what happens to officers in the later stages of their career, once they establish themselves after the first few years. Presumably changes in assignment, rank, and the like would have further effects on officer behavior, and misconduct more specifically.

This focus on the early years of police service is due to a number of studies indicating that early organizational learning is a major determinant of one's later organizational beliefs, attitudes, and behav-

---

3. This hypothesis seems largely misguided as it seeks to demonstrate that police are psychologically homogeneous and somehow different from the general public. It seems more plausible to look at variation among police with high and low levels of authoritarianism, and observe differences in their behavior (Worden, 1996).

iors (van Maanen, 1973). While some degree of socialization occurs at all career stages, it seems that the organization is most persuasive during career entry because newcomers have few guidelines to direct their behavior. It therefore seems plausible to focus one's research efforts into early socialization. Moreover, the police culture is often characterized as monolithic, and therefore all police become more-or-less uniform in their beliefs, attitudes, and (presumably) behaviors over time. As van Maanen (1975) writes, "the police culture can be viewed as molding attitudes—with numbing regularity—of virtually all who enter" (p. 215). While somewhat limiting in scope, this body of research offers some intriguing hypotheses for the development of a career framework of police misconduct.

Researchers such as van Maanen's (1973), with his nine-month participant observation study on police socialization in Union City in 1970, and Fielding's (1984), in his year-long work following Derbyshire police recruits in 1980, propose a four-stage model for the socialization process. The first stage, the "choice" (van Maanen, 1973) or "pre-entry" (Fielding, 1984) stage, deals with the sort of people attracted to a police career, and their initial occupational expectations. Much of the research here fails to support the "authoritarian syndrome" which was previously ascribed to such persons (McNamara, 1967; Sterling, 1972, van Maanen, 1973) and instead supports the contention that police careers are considered by potential candidates as one job among many, and along the same dimension of any other job choice. It seems that recruits come in with a variety of experience, some related to law enforcement (e.g., military police, police aides, security personnel), and others with no experience at all. They also come in with a host of general notions about the nature of police work, some more idealistic than practical (Hopper, 1977). Generally at this stage, the individuals who have yet to take the oath of office see the police department in its most favorable light, and have high expectations for their future career.

The next stage, the "admittance" or "introduction" stage, focuses on the probationary period where the new recruit attends the police academy. For many, this is the newcomer's first contact with the police subculture, and is, as described by some researchers, a "reality shock" (Niederhoffer, 1967; van Maanen, 1973; Westley, 1970). Persons embarking on their policing career quickly move from being a person who has "made it" on the job to a probationary member of the force who can be removed at any time (van Maanen, 1974). Placed with other probationary members, the new recruit quickly learns the harsh discipline of the police academy. The academy is characterized by "absolute adherence to departmental rules, rigorous physical training, dull lectures ... and a ritualistic concern for detail" (van Maanen, 1973, p. 89). Niederhoffer (1967), in his observations of the New York City Police Academy, remarks "For two months the recruit ... is cut off from the rest of the department and overwhelmed by a mountain of study, most of it complex and demanding ... At the academy he masters ... the web of protocol and ceremony that characterizes any quasi-military hierarchy" (p. 42). This is not to say that the entire training is formal. In fact, many police academy trainers share their "war stories" about what real police work is like, and thus provide recruits with even more grist to develop a collective understanding of police work.

While certainly a trying time for the recruit, it is also a time to learn and change. Indeed, it appears that some recruits, once obtaining more information on the functioning of police work, find that it is incongruent with their initial expectations. Such recruits deal with this cognitive dissonance by either adopting a different (and presumably more realistic) perspective, or leave the academy (Hoper, 1977). Those who stay certainly begin to alter their high expectations of police work due to the stress placed upon them at the academy, and they learn the lesson that if the department notices their behavior, it is usually to administer a punishment (Fielding, 1984; van Maanen, 1974). Moskos (2008), who spent twenty months policing Baltimore's eastern district, wrote "the academy is not a 'weed-out' process. The academy is less a learning process than a ritualized hazing to be endured" (p. 21).

Once done with academy training, the rookies are sent out to be seasoned in the field. This stage, known as the "encounter" or "change" phase of development, is where the newcomer is introduced to the complexities of actual police work through their Field

Training Officer (FTO). The FTO is typically a veteran officer with several years of experience, and becomes, "the single most important person in shaping the behavior of the novice" (van Maanen, 1974, p. 91). It is through their FTO that rookie police officers learn what is expected of a patrolperson within the police milieu.

This phase represents an important period of "apprenticeship-like socialization" (van Maanen, 1973) where the rookie learns the ins and outs of fieldwork, and begins to understand the difference between academy training and "real police work." The newcomer, during the initial tours of patrol, is likely to feel ill-prepared for the day-to-day tasks of police patrol. While they have knowledge of the criminal code, arrest procedures, etc, they are unsure of their practical application. They learn the ropes through their initial months on patrol, both by watching and listening to their FTO, and by participating in a number of common police activities, all the while being evaluated by the FTO and other officers. For many neophytes, this is another time of "reality shock," where recruits experience first-hand the "vast discrepancy between idealistic expectations and sordid reality" (Neiderhoffer, 1967, p. 49).

It is at this phase that recruits are most susceptible to attitude change. Since the recruit learns rapidly that academy training has not prepared them adequately for patrolwork, they seek behavioral guidelines through "police folklore": tales, myths, and legends communicated to the recruit by other officers and their FTO (van Maanen, 1973). It is through these stories that rookies begin to adopt the perspectives of their more experienced colleagues.

It is also here that the newcomer must resolve a dilemma between adopting the approach of professionalism stressed by the academy, or the more pragmatic approach adopted by patrolpersons on the street (Neiderhoffer, 1967). In fact, when compared with academy training, the informal socialization that occurs during the "change" phase has been referred to as "counter training," and has been linked to the development of police misconduct (Bahn, 1975; Sherman, 1974). Moskos (2008) notes that in the academy, trainees were actively kept away from patrol officers, as they were seen by the administration not as mentors, but as potentially corrupting influences. One might suppose that when officers are learning the ropes and are struggling to discover behavioral guidelines to survive on patrol, they can pick up or develop poor work habits from an unskilled FTO or their peer group more generally. This would be especially problematic in agencies that are not careful in their FTO selection (see, for example, Independent Commission on the Los Angeles Police Department, 1991).

In fact, Sherman (1974) describes in detail how an officer, through a process of affiliation with other police officers, can come to engage in corruption through a series of moral choices over the course of his or her career. For Sherman, the process of becoming a police officer includes a set of contingencies that produce moral experiences in officers that change their frames of reference. The key contingency as to whether an officer will become corrupt (defined in Sherman's work as becoming a grafter or a police burglar) is the work group to which the rookie is assigned. Based on a collection of case studies, Sherman argues that officers learn to be grafters through a series of moral choices about the social harm in taking graft, and a series of neutralizations regarding that harm as they continue through a series of stages to increasingly lucrative—but morally objectionable—payoffs.

The series starts with the acceptance of free coffee or meals from restaurants on their beat. These perks usually begin early in a rookie's career, and the peer pressure to accept them is great. As the officer becomes used to accepting these small perks, he or she has a different self image, allowing him/her to continue down a road of continual acceptance of greater perks: a bar owner offers the officer free drinks to be allowed to stay open after closing hours, a motorist hands the officer a bribe to avoid a ticket, a construction foreman gives the officer money to overlook materials left illegally on a sidewalk, etc. (Sherman, 1974). If an officer accepts these minor payoffs, he/she proves capable of accepting more regular forms of graft, and senior officers who receive regular payoffs from gamblers, prostitutes, etc., may offer the newer police officer a cut of the money if he/she desires. While an officer can refuse to engage in graft, or additional graft once started, it is interesting to see how new officers can be encouraged into a career of graft through a process of affiliation with other officers as they progress through the "encounter" or "change" phase.

Besides moral choices regarding corruption, other aspects of informal socialization can encourage other types of misconduct. Rookies may learn that some types of people do not warrant police protection, or that some types of people should be responded to frequently with coercion. As Barker (1991) writes, "the largest acts of police brutality are the result of occupational socialization ... The police peer group may define excessive use of force as acceptable in certain circumstances; such as to command respect from an unruly prisoner, to obtain information, to punish certain classes of deviants (sex criminals, hardened criminals) or classes of perceived deviants ('hippies,' radicals, hillbillies, punk kids, etc.)" (p. 127). Indeed, rookie police officers are quickly taught to dominate and take control of citizen encounters, and to respond punitively to persons who refuse to recognize police authority. People who disrespect the police, question their authority, or refuse to take them seriously are labeled with terms like "wise guys" (Westley, 1970) or "assholes" (van Maanen, 1978), and police consider it appropriate to use coercion or force against such citizens in order to gain deference. According to van Maanen (1978), the informal norms of police permit the application of street justice to the "asshole," in the form of a "thumping" with charges of disorderly conduct or resisting arrest filed in order to construct a legally justified account of the interaction.

This type of force is differentiated by Hunt (1985), who argues that some forms of illegal force (as defined by the courts) are considered normal by police. This type of "normal force" involves acts of coercion that police see as necessary, appropriate, and reasonable under certain circumstances, but would be labeled excessive by the public (Hunt, 1985). Such normal force is still different from police brutality, which is considered to exceed working police notions of normal force. For Hunt, the idea of "normal force" is not learned in the academy, but during a rookie's early experiences. In fact, Hunt suggests that rookies are commended for using normal force when appropriate, but can still be reprimanded (mostly on an informal basis) for brutality.

In some respects, this process is similar to the moral/ethical slope traveled by officers who become involved in corruption described previously. Rookie officers learn from their associations with more experienced patrolpersons that some citizens are to be responded to with coercion, and this type of force is normal and expected if an officer is to control encounters with these types of people. If an officer accepts these norms regarding coercion, they may increasingly become comfortable with using force more generally to solve problems with citizens, especially any who display disrespect towards an officer's authority. It may even be the case that some officers become more sensitive to displays of disrespect, increasingly interpreting even some innocuous behaviors as signs of disrespect, and responding to such with coercion. Again, as noted before, an officer can refuse to engage in this type of behavior, or refuse to apply coercion more widely once he/she has started to use it against certain types of people, but such behavior is formed initially during the "encounter" or "change" phase through a process of affiliation with other officers.

In addition to adopting police folklore and informal training, the rookie police officer undergoes a set of important experiences that not only constitutes a practical learning process, but also serves to develop the officer's reputation regarding how well he or she measures up to the demands of patrolwork. It is from these early experiences that the subcultural norms of police work are transmitted (van Maanen, 1974). It is important to note here that it is experience, not academy training, which shapes a police neophyte's behavior and outlooks. In fact, research into the informal organization of police culture has suggested that a rookie's first few contacts with the public can have a tremendous impact on how he or she later approaches similar situations (Neiderhoffer, 1967; van Maanen, 1975).

While shown a certain amount of lenience for mistakes during the first few months, new officers are nevertheless judged on how they handle a number of varying situations. The FTO and other officers are especially interested in how the rookie will handle "hot" calls (van Maanen, 1975). Generally, these calls represent situations that may result in bodily harm to the officer: calls like "bar brawl," "man-with-gun," or "robbery in-progress." These calls represent what experienced officers consider "real police work" and how one handles such calls are in a very real sense the measure of an officer (van Maanen, 1973). About such experiences, van Maanen (1973) writes, "while such calls are relatively rare on a day-to-day basis, their occurrence signals a behavioral test of the recruit ... By placing himself in a vulnerable position and pluckily backing-up his FTO and/or other patrolmen, a recruit demonstrates his inclination to share the risks of police work. Through such events, a newcomer quickly makes a departmental reputation which will follow him for the remainder of his career" (p. 413).

This is not to say that rushing off to calls or pushing eagerly for action is always admirable. Rookies who are always looking for tasks to perform are accosted by veterans for having a "gung-ho" attitude (van Maanen, 1974). Many veterans seek to spend as much time as possible off the street, expressing the fact that one can "get into trouble out there" (van Maanen, 1974). This is not meant to imply that officers who seek to stay out of trouble do nothing. "Laying low" is sharply distinguished from "loafing." Experienced officers seek to cover their district and answer dispatched calls, but in essence, they seek little more than to do what is assigned of them in an attempt to avoid trouble. Some researchers have noted that "laying low" can also be conceived of as more than doing the least amount of work possible. Instead, a more active approach to "laying low" would be for officers to focus their attention on situations that are less ambiguous (e.g., serious offenses) (Terrill et al., 2003). This allows officers to lay-low while adhering to the crime-fighting mandate popular within the police subculture.

The final phase is labeled the "metamorphosis" or "continuance" phase. It is at this time that police rookies end their period under the supervision of a FTO and are assigned to a permanent precinct, thus shedding their "trainee" status. With their "reality shock" and early formative experiences behind them, these officers now have several months invested into their police career. They begin to settle into their job, adjusting to the relatively monotonous, slow-moving pace of police work.

In short, new officers learn that what initially attracted them to police work (that the work would be exciting and dramatic) is largely false; such activities are few and far between. Since most of the officer's time is spent on tasks other than responding to "hot calls," there is little incentive for performance. In fact, in his study of Union City police, van Maanen (1975) found that motivation on the job declined over time. This was largely due to an overall decrease in expectancies of rewards for working hard. The officer discovers that the best way to negotiate day-to-day police work is to stay out of trouble. As Bayley and Bittner (1984) write, "Police, unlike workers in most other jobs, are constantly being reminded of the fatefulness of their actions to themselves as well as to the public. They believe their jobs are on the line daily. So for police to avoid what would be viewed as a mistake by the department ... is imperative" (p. 43). To do this, the officer minimizes the set of activities he/she pursues, and in many ways behaves like his/her more experienced colleagues.

How long it takes officers on average to settle into the policing role has not been specified in the policing literature. Police scholars have argued that policing is a craft, and as such most of what is learned in policing occurs in the field across years of experience, not in their training academies or in subsequent training seminars. Bayley and Bittner (1984) argue that the valuable lessons officers learn through the haphazard mechanism of individual experience concerns "the goals of policing—which are reasonable; tactics—which ones ensure achievement of different goals in varying circumstances; and presence—how to cultivate a career-sustaining personality" (p. 51). The duration required for officers to learn these valuable lessons remains unknown, and certainly officers will vary in the time it takes to do so.[4] Some police psychologists suggest that officers fully mature after about the fifth or sixth year of experience, but are most likely to engage in problem behaviors until then (Mered-

---

4. Moskos (2008) notes that his learning curve seemed to flatten-out after about a year (p. 194).

ith, 1986). While interesting to note, there is little systematic data on the relationship between experience and misconduct. The point of discussing the police socialization process is to emphasize the changes officers experience over time. One can see from this literature that people who plunge into the process of becoming an officer are certainly changed by the time they emerge. Their experience with the police academy, their first few months with their FTO, and their adjustment to their first assignment all lead officers to change and adapt to their work environment—for better or for worse. Officers' initial experiences on the street are formative, and in handling such situations, officers gradually adopt the "working personality" of other officers as a means of handling the occupational challenges of police work. After some time on the job, younger officers learn to lay low so as to not attract unwanted attention from the department. Unfortunately, motivation and commitment to the police organization also decrease over time, and officers generally become more cynical about the job (Neiderhoffer, 1967; van Maanen, 1975), even while they increase in their ability to manage police work effectively (Bayley & Bittner, 1984).

From this summary of the police socialization literature, one can derive a number of developmentally-related hypotheses regarding misconduct. First, one would expect rookie police officers to be more "gung ho" than their more experienced colleagues, making them more likely to engage in larger amounts of police activity, and by implication, more likely to get into trouble with citizens. Research supports this contention. For example, Friedrich's (1977) reanalysis of the Black-Reiss data found that less experienced officers do more to detect crime: they initiate more citizen contacts, do more active patrolling, and record more crime reports from citizens when compared to officers with more experience. Additionally Worden (1989), in his analysis of the PSS data, found that more experienced officers made fewer traffic and suspicion stops. Crank (1993) also finds support for this hypothesis in his study of eight municipal police departments in Illinois. He finds that police officers with more time in service are less likely to engage in order-maintenance or legalistic behaviors.

Second, one expects that officers will increase in their skills related to police work, and this, combined with less activity, should result in fewer mistakes by the officer that eventuate in citizen complaints, except possibly in situations where citizens do not defer to police authority. To the extent that activity and use of force are related, one might expect that police would be less apt to resort to force as they gain in experience and their activity levels decline. But a different hypothesis might be derived as well. One might expect that officers will continually encounter "assholes" on the job, and will tend to use force against such persons. Additionally, since the potentially dangerous "hot calls" are important to police (i.e., they are seen as "real police work"), and are likely to result in a use of force incident, one might not expect veteran officers to stop using force completely, but perhaps reach a consistently low rate, as they use force only on a reactive basis in a limited number of circumstances.

The literature here is mixed, and it is difficult to say for certain whether experience matters in the extent to which officers use force. For example, Worden (1996) finds that length of service has no effect on the use of either reasonable or excessive force, but Garner et al. (1996) found that experience was an "inconsistent" predictor of force. Terrill and Mastrofski (2002), in their analysis of the Project on Policing Neighborhoods (POPN) data, find that less experienced officers were more likely to use all types of force, including verbal commands and threats, physical restraint, and impact methods, when compared to more experienced officers (see also Paoline and Terrill, 2007). McElvain and Kposowa (2004) found that officers with five to nine years of experience were twelve times more likely to have been investigated by internal affairs for an alleged improper use of force than those with twenty of more years of experience. Experience has also been shown to be important in the use of deadly force as well, with research by Alpert (1989) and Blumberg (1982) demonstrating that inexperienced officers use deadly force more often than their experienced colleagues.

There is also mixed support for the hypothesis that force is more likely against suspects who are disrespectful. This proposition emerged with early qualitative police research (van Maanen, 1974,

1978; Westley, 1970), but scholars question whether such research is generalizable since it was based on one agency, at one point in time, and is largely impressionistic. Later studies based upon systematic observations of police have repeatedly found that the demeanor of suspects is one of the more important factors in their treatment by police (Worden et al., 1996). Subjects who are disrespectful or non-compliant with the police are more likely to be subject of police disrespect, physical force, and arrest (Mastrofski et al., 2002; Reiss 1971; Worden & Shepard, 1996).

However, some have called these research findings into question, arguing that the concept of demeanor has not been adequately measured by quantitative research, and other important variables (e.g., criminal behavior of suspects) are not controlled in these analyses (Klinger, 1994). Of particular interest here is the possible confounding of suspect disrespect and suspect resistance. Suspects in a police-citizen encounter can engage in disrespect towards the police by expressing their displeasure with an officer's understanding of the situation, but this does not mean they were at all resistant. However, citizens who express their displeasure while also refusing to comply with an officer's command are both resistant and disrespectful. Analyses of the citizen demeanor could take both of these situations and place them under the rubric of "defying police authority," but for testing the hypothesis that force is more likely against disrespectful subjects, it would prove useful to separate these two. This would enable one to differentiate the independent effects that both suspect resistance and suspect disrespect have on the likelihood that police use force.

Some empirical work has been able to incorporate this criticism and utilize more careful analyses when it comes to examining suspect demeanor in police-citizen encounters. For example, Worden and Shepard (1996), in a reanalysis of the 1977 Police Services Study, find that previous results from these data still hold—a hostile demeanor is an important predictor of police behavior and is not contingent on how it is measured, even with the inclusion of more adequate controls. Mastrofski et al. (2002), using the POPN data from 1996–1997, found that suspect initiation of disrespect to be significant in determining whether the police themselves were disrespectful, controlling for other variables such as suspect resistance. Suspect resistance itself was not significant in explaining police disrespect towards citizens.

Interestingly, Terrill and Mastrofski (2002), using the same POPN data set, find that suspect disrespect *is not* significant in determining police coercion. Suspect resistance, on the other hand, *is* a significant variable in explaining police coercion. This study is important in that not only can it distinguish suspect resistance from suspect disrespect, but it also considers a wide range of police use of force: from verbal commands and threats to different applications of physical force (i.e., physical restraint and impact methods).

Terrill & Mastrofski (2002) recognize that their findings regarding suspect disrespect diverge from previous research and offer two explanations. First, their ability to clearly distinguish suspect resistance and suspect disrespect towards the police affords an opportunity to analyze the two separately. This was something which most previous research was unable to accomplish, and so the two were often improperly meshed. Second, the finding that a suspect's disrespect did not contribute to police coercion may be linked to changes in policing (Fyfe, 1996). Policing has undergone considerable changes (e.g., changes in criminal laws, administrative policies, and civil protections) since the early observational police research, which took place between the mid-1960s and the mid-1970s, and these changes have limited police discretion in citizen encounters (Terrill & Mastrofski, 2002).

Overall it appears that some of the hypotheses derived from the socialization literature received support from subsequent research. Officers become less productive with age, and experience can play a role in the likelihood that officers resort to using force. While it appears that contemporary police officers do not use force unnecessarily against disrespectful citizens, they are still likely to use force against subjects who resist police authority. Moreover, citizen disrespect appears to prompt police disrespect, and the latter is still a form of misconduct worthy of study. These findings are important when one considers police officer misconduct careers in the aggregate, which are discussed below.

The Experience-Misconduct Curve

The above discussion illustrates a singular process for the development of police deviance. To summarize: rookies are often anxious to prove themselves to other officers, and are thus rather "gung-ho" when compared to more experienced officers who have adopted a "lay low" approach. As the rookies gain street experience and are eventually assigned to a permanent beat, they too adopt a "lay low" perspective, and therefore avoid all work except that which is required of them, all the while presumably gaining in skill while mastering the craft of policing. If this is largely accurate, one would expect, plotting a chart using years of experience and some measure of officer misconduct, to find a stable, meaningful relationship. Specifically, one would expect to find that officers very early in their careers (i.e., while at the academy) to engage in very little misconduct because they have little contact with patrol officers or citizens. Once on the street under the supervision of an FTO, one would expect more problem behaviors as rookie officers are learning the ropes, and are expected to "prove themselves." The amount of deviance is expected to increase over the next few months, as rookie officers seek to earn a positive reputation amongst their fellow officers and begin to adopt the work practices (both good and bad) of their peers. Eventually, officers leave the supervision of their FTOs and are assigned to a precinct and squad. This may happen relatively quickly, or it may take months. While existing research does not provide one with an estimate of how long it takes relatively new officers to adopt a "lay low" approach or increase in the essential police skills through experience, one can presume officers will continue to make mistakes and learn over the course of the next few years as they move through their "adolescent phase" and begin to master their craft. As officers are continually socialized (i.e., develop their "working personality") and presumably decrease their proactive police work, the officer will engage in less misconduct, and eventually plateau out or desist entirely. One might also expect this decline from officer maturation and life events outside of police work that grants them a greater stake in conformity (e.g., marriage, children, a mortgage, etc.). The exact timing of these different elements is difficult to pinpoint based on the existing literature, but one should see *at the aggregate level* a sharp increase in problem behaviors in the early years of police experience, a plateau of this misconduct sometime within the first few years, and then a gradual decrease as members are socialized and gain in skill.[5]

Possible Trajectories of Police Misconduct

If experience and misconduct are related in an orderly way in the aggregate, this does not necessarily imply that each and every officer will follow this pattern. Some certainly may, but others might follow a path different from the one used to describe the average trend in these behaviors for all officers. Chapter 1 notes that criminologists found the existence of an aggregate age-crime curve, but that this aggregate pattern did not always hold at the individual level. Is there evidence in the policing literature that one might draw upon to predict patterns of misconduct that would deviate from the aggregate curve? Up to this point, examination of the police research has focused on the aspects of occupational socialization which emphasizes similarities in officers' adaptation to the to the police role over its variation. But many have come to question the notion of a singular police culture, and have suggested that there are differ-

---

5. Note that this pattern is for nondeviant organizations, or police departments where behaviors like corruption or brutality is not commonplace or encouraged. Members of deviant agencies would have an aggregate career patterns much different from relatively nondeviant departments, especially with regards to career dimensions such as frequency and overall participation.

ing ways in which police officers cope with, and adjust to, the unique demands of police work.[6]

There is some research which suggests that "the" police culture has been changing due to the influx of officers with a college education, a change in the demography of police organizations with the hiring of more female and minority officers, and the advent of shifting police priorities (e.g., community policing) (Bahn, 1984). Others have also noted the socialization process does not necessarily result in attitudinal homogeneity (Bennett, 1984; Worden, 1993). As such, police scholars such as Brown (1988), Muir (1977) and others have developed police typologies (or, to use Brown's term, "operational styles") based upon the varying views officers have of their occupational roles, restrictions to their legal authority, use of coercion, the status of their clientele, etc. (see Worden, 1995). Unfortunately, these typologies are not designed to explain officer behavior, and do not discuss misconduct directly. Moreover, police typologies do not specifically consider these types within a developmental framework, so it is difficult to say whether officers switch types over the course of their career, or whether particular types are even sustainable over the long-term given the nature of police work.[7]

There is one typology worth discussing here as it deals directly with officer misconduct. The work of Scrivner (1994) formulates five officer types based on a specific kind of misconduct — use of excessive force. Not based on attitudes or psychological dimensions, Scrivner's types are instead distilled from characteristics of

---

6. Many question whether there was a dominant police culture to begin with. As Worden (1995) writes, "Whether or to what extent the police officers of the 1960s conformed to the police personality are questions that apparently ceased to interest scholars before they were conclusively answered" (p. 50).

7. Brown (1988) does note that police aggressiveness tended to drop sharply between two and four years of experience in his study, and suspected that officers who exhibit a highly aggressive style shift towards a less aggressive style after five years (p. 244).

officers referred to police psychologists for excessive force. The data, derived from police psychologists replying to Scrivner's survey, was used to construct these five distinct police profiles. These profiles are beneficial to the current discussion in that they point to specific causal mechanisms for misconduct, and do not develop out of an understanding of varying police attitudes which may or may not impact actual behaviors. However, such officer profiles are based on the impressions of psychologists treating police officers, and not direct observations or surveys of the officers themselves.

The first profile discussed by Scrivner was of officers with personality disorders that place them at chronic risk for excessive use of force. Such officers have personality traits that are manifested in antisocial and abusive tendencies, interfering with judgment and interactions with citizens. These conditions are especially volatile when the officer perceives challenges to his or her authority, which, as was previously noted, places citizens at risk for having force used against them. These personality characteristics tend to persist throughout life, but may be intensified by police work. Such personality patterns create persons who generally do not learn from experience or accept responsibility for their behavior, and therefore are at risk for repeated complaints. Out of the five profiles, Scrivner indicates that this is the smallest in number of the high-risk groups.

The second profile consists of officers whose previous job-related experiences place them at risk for excessive force. Unlike the first group, these officers are not unsocialized, egocentric, or violent. Their vulnerability to excessive force instead stems from "emotional baggage" they have accumulated from pervious traumatic incidents such as justifiable police shootings. Typically, these officers suffer from burnout and are socially isolated from their squads. Because of their perceived need to hide their symptoms from other officers, a good deal of time can elapse before the officer's problem comes to light. When it does happen, it is usually the result of an excessive force situation in which the officer has lost control.

The third profile sounds very familiar: officers who have problems at the early stages of their careers. This profile consists of young, inexperienced officers who are seen as "hotdogs," "badge happy," or "macho" (Scrivner, 1994). These officers, while bringing positive attributes to the job, are nevertheless characterized as impulsive with a low tolerance for frustration. But, as the early socialization research suggests and Scrivner also notes, these officers tend to outgrow these tendencies and learn from experience.

The fourth at-risk officer is one who develops inappropriate patrol styles. These individuals, "combine a dominant command presence with a heavy-handed policing style; they are particularly sensitive to challenge and provocation" (Scrivner, 1994). Such officers use force to demonstrate that they are in charge, and as they continue in this behavior, it becomes the norm. An important implication of this profile is that such officers learn this behavior on the job, and is not the result of pre-entry personality disorders. One has already seen how informal socialization can encourage aggressive stances with citizens, especially those who fail to display the adequate amount of deference to police authority. It seems that this officer profile deeply internalizes this norm to the point where it causes severe problems in police-citizen encounters.

The fifth and final profile of the officer at-risk for excessive force is one with personal problems. These problems destabilize the officer's job functioning by undermining the officer's ability to cope with fear, animosity, and emotionally charged police situations. Generally these officers exhibit no signs of abuse of force before the problem occurs, and can usually be identified before they resort to excessive force by their erratic behavior. Scrivner indicates that this is the largest group, and the most widely-referred to police psychologists.

Besides the work of Scrivner, there is one other officer type that deals specifically with misconduct — the problem officer. Like the criminological literature, research on police misconduct has found that a small percent of the officer population (around 5–10%) accounts for a disproportionate share of all officer misconduct (referring here mostly to excessive force). If this is the case, then perhaps there is a career deviant in the police world whose behavior is persistent and enduring, much like Moffitt's (1993) Life-Course Persistent offender, or, more appropriately, Scrivner's first profile of an officer with antisocial personality traits. It may also be that the rest of the police behave much like the police socialization literature would lead us to expect: an officer whose misconduct looks much like the aggregate experience-misconduct curve in the way Moffit's Adolescent Limited offender (normatively) follows the age-crime curve. This would also leave a number of officers who belong to a "nonoffending" or "abstainer" population: officers who never engage in any misconduct over their careers.

The difficulty with problem officers is that the concept implies stability in deviance over time (barring intervention or termination), but existing research only provides a brief window into an officer's career. Problem officers are typically identified as those exceeding some threshold of citizen complaints (e.g., three complaints in a single year), and as such finds these officers to be male, young, and inexperienced (Brandl et al., 2001; Lersch and Mieczkowski, 1996; McElvain and Kposowa, 2004). In short, problem officers are found where the experience-misconduct curve is expected to be at its peak. This being the case, one is concerned with officer heterogeneity. Identifying problem officers using a short time span and during the point at which aggregate misconduct is at its peak, one may be selecting a group of officers with very different careers ahead of them. Some of these officers may certainly be continually problematic, but others may be only episodically problematic. Current research—and EI Systems as well—assume problem officers identified in a given time period will continue to be problematic in later time periods, since their behavior is thought to be tied to some enduring antisocial trait unlikely to change, thus implying their behavior is rather static over time. Yet this assumption has never been tested, which leads one to question the entire concept of a problem officer. It may be that all or most problem officers desist from their problem behaviors after they grow out of their "adolescent phase," as do the officers described in Scrivner's third profile.

Investigating this question is easier if one adopts a developmental perspective. In doing so, one characterizes the problem officer in terms of their misconduct career elements. Thus, problem officers, if their behavior is tied to a persistent antisocial trait, would exhibit an earlier onset, a higher frequency, and a longer duration of problem behaviors when compared to other less problematic or non-problem officers. The continuity of this behavior remains in question however, since research has yet to examine the careers of problem officers. Given that problem officer behavior is rooted in some antisocial trait, it is unlikely to be on par with that of other deviants. Moreover, officers who garner a large number of citizen complaints are likely to be more closely monitored by their supervisors, punished for their misdeeds, and perhaps reassigned, thus limiting opportunities for deviance and providing a state dependent effect which mitigates against future misconduct.

Also, as Lersch (2002) has noted, using citizen complaints as a primary indicator of misconduct brings about methodological difficulties in addition to the conceptual difficulties noted above. She has posited a "good apples" hypothesis, stating that citizen complaints are more of a byproduct of proactive police work and not a good measure of an underlying tendency to engage in problem behaviors. As such, problem officers are not really problems at all, but proactive officers out there earning their paychecks. The research here has been limited and the results mixed, with Lersch (2002) finding measures of officer productivity to be weakly-to-moderately correlated to the number of citizen complaints an officer receives. Terrill and McCluskey (2002) have found that problem officers were more likely to engage in proactive field stops, but were also more likely to use physical force than non-problem officers, suggesting that active officers are both productive *and* problematic. Such findings suggest that citizen complaints are related to productivity, but also to the levels of coercion officers employ in their contact with citizens (see also McCluskey and Terrill, 2005). Research in this vein illustrates the difficulty in measuring misconduct via citizen complaints, since some officers can behave well in a contact with a citizen, yet still have a complaint file against them, either by a citizen who does not understand correct police procedure, or one who seeks to gain a legal advantage over the officer (e.g., in the case of an arrest). It is unclear, given current research, whether arrests lead to complaints, or whether the use of force led to arrests to "cover" its illegitimate use (Brandl et al., 2001).

In sum, it may be that the officers who are defined as problematic based on some predefined threshold captures a group of inexperienced officers who have very different careers ahead of them. By identifying and capturing problem officers at the peak of the experience-misconduct curve, where misconduct heterogeneity is at its peak, one captures officers whose misconduct may be "adolescent-limited" to their early years and no later. It is entirely unclear whether such problem officers identified early in their careers will be "life-course persistent" (i.e., enduringly problematic), leading one to question whether the notion of problem officers is sustainable across careers. Such a vital investigation into the career patterns of these officers has not yet been undertaken.

The essential point here is that *while at the aggregate level there may exist a general "experience-misconduct" curve, within that curve there may exist distinct officer career trajectories.* Much like the research that has identified distinct criminal career paths discussed in Chapter 1, based on the relatively sparse policing literature, one might presuppose the existence of differing career paths in police misconduct. First, one might propose that a group of officers follows a career path similar to the aggregate curve. A second group would follow a problem officer career path, with an earlier onset, higher frequency, and a longer duration of problem behaviors than the first group. Whether or not this group desists (or when) remains to be seen. Besides these two groups, both of which are problematic in terms of their behavior, a third group, which is not problematic, could be posed. This group would be an abstainer group who does not engage in problem behaviors or for whom these behaviors are extremely limited.

However, one must allow for the possibility that officers follow a general experience-misconduct path at the individual level as well, meaning that there may exist only one career trajectory. Here, officers engage in minor misconduct early in their career, but increase in skill with experience. This, combined with the development of a lay-low attitude, leads to less misconduct at later career stages. The rest of the variation in misconduct around this central career path may occur when an officer develops personal problems, as Scrivner's fifth profile suggests. A developmental perspective allows one to explore these questions empirically, and will go beyond consideration of career deviants such as problem officers and allows for the possibility that other career trajectories may exist.

The Advantages of Using a Developmental Framework

The problem with problem officers is the lack of a common set of terms to characterize police misconduct over time. Besides the observation that a small number of officers account for a sizable portion of citizen complaints (typically for excessive force), police researchers do not yet have a framework for identifying or examining problem officers, and implicitly assume problem officers are static in their career course. Moreover, as is argued above, the literature hints at the possibility of differing career paths in terms of misconduct over the course of an officer's career, but researchers lack a cohesive lexicon and framework for characterizing these career paths. By applying the terms and concepts described in Chapter 1, police misconduct can be considered from a developmental perspective.

Employing criminal career terminology, concepts in the literature on developmental criminology, and the risk factor prevention paradigm as ways of thinking about police misconduct has several advantages. First, it encourages thinking of police misconduct in terms of temporal, within-individual change. Very little existing research considers police behavior over time, and those studies that do still rely on cross-sectional comparisons between officers, or examine the behavior or attitudes of officers over short time periods. Second, using a developmental or career perspective will encourage the identification of events that may affect misconduct. While existing research identifies causes of police misconduct from sociological, psychological, and organizational frameworks (Worden, 1995), using a developmental perspective allows one to also consider life events and their impact on different career paths. Third, one might begin to develop officer typologies based on developmental considerations, identifying causes of misconduct and considering how such causes would affect different dimensions of a misconduct career such as onset, frequency, duration, and desistance. Finally, the utilization of a developmental model of police misconduct will also allow consideration of the consequences of misconduct in addition to its causes.

There are few studies of police that are longitudinal in nature, meaning that there are few studies that consider temporal, within-individual change. The studies that do exist cover attitude changes of officers over time, mostly at the beginning of their careers. Such studies as those by van Maanen (1975) and Fielding (1988) discussed previously, utilize a sample population of one academy class, and follow them for their first few years of their career. These studies demonstrate that considerable attitude change accompanies the experience of becoming a police officer, but little work has been done to cover misconduct specifically. Also mentioned earlier, these studies are often qualitative in nature and use small samples, thereby limiting their generalizability.

Other studies that do examine forms of misconduct such as excessive force or disrespect towards citizens examine differences between large groups of officers at one point in time, increasing its generalizability. Thus, by examining correlates or factors thought to be associated with misconduct, such studies compare rookies to more experienced officers, or officers with college education to officers without such education. Hence, investigations into police misconduct examine only between-individual change. For example, the research on problem officers discussed above compares officers identified as problematic during a short time period to officers who were not problematic, assuming those individuals selected as problematic will continue to be so over their career course.

Currently, no study examines police misconduct in individual officers over their career course, so researchers do not have estimations of the average year of onset for problem behaviors (although the literature hints that it would tend to be early), or the average frequency with which officers are involved in instances of misconduct over their career course, or the average duration of an officer's career in misconduct, or how it changes over time more generally. There are, however, some estimations of participation, especially in the use of force, but these estimations involve use of force *across encounters*, not officers. For example, Craft (1985) analyzed use of force reports completed by officers in Rochester, New York. For a six year period, the police completed nearly 2,400 use-of-force reports and made over 123,000 arrests. The ratio of arrests to incidents of force was 52 to 1. Observational studies show that use of force is also rare. For example, Freidrich (1980), in an observational study of police in three cities in 1966, found that police used force in 5 percent of their encounters with suspected offenders. Similar percentages were found in observations of police in New York City (Bayley and Garafalo, 1989) and in the Police Services Study, which comprised an examination of 24 police departments (Worden, 1995). Sykes and Brent (1980) analyzed interactions between officers and citizens and also concluded that "coercive regulation [including threats as well as the actual use of force] is rare" (p. 195).

Some studies have even attempted to estimate the prevalence of improper force across encounters, which is more relevant to the present topic of inquiry.[8] Reiss (1968) and Freidrich (1980), using the same data from police observations in three cities in 1966, found that improper force was used in no more than 2.5 percent of their encounters with offenders. Worden (1995) found that improper force was used in only 1.3 percent of police encounters with suspects observed in the 1977 Police Services Study. Given that police use force very infrequently, and that the prevalence of improper force is even more infrequent, one might expect that any given officer will have

---

8. Of course, one would rather have estimates of prevalence across officers over time.

few incidents of force (especially improper force) over the course of their career (i.e., one would expect a low frequency).

Borrowing from the risk factor prevention paradigm, very few examinations of police misconduct consider risk or protective factors that may affect misconduct. The literature certainly points to some events that could be considered risk factors for an increase in misconduct, such as assignment to a high-crime area (Kane, 2002) or exposure to other officers who engage in a high degree of misconduct (Sherman, 1974), but it is often not couched in developmental terms. There is no consideration as to how these risk factors might differentially affect an officer's onset, frequency, duration, or desistance. In addition, little to no attempt has been made to examine other risk factors known to predict antisocial behavior found in criminological studies.

The risk factors that have been considered tie into research on officer demographic (e.g., race) and background characteristics (e.g., education). For example, Freidrich (1980) found that Black officers patrol more aggressively, initiate more contacts with citizens, and make more arrests. Also, other research has shown that male officers tend to initiate more encounters and make more arrests than females officers (Sherman, 1975). Education has been shown to have little effect on officer arrest behavior, but more educated officers have been found to be at a decreased risk of citizen complaints (Worden, 1990) and to use less verbal and physical force (Paoline and Terrill, 2007). Fyfe (2002) found that military experience may be related to the likelihood of dismissal from a police force for misconduct. In his study of 1,543 officers who were involuntarily separated from the NYPD between 1975 and 1996 and a comparison sample of their academy classmates, the author found that officers with military experience were more likely to be involuntarily separated than those officers without such experience.

This research, combined with the research on experience and police behavior, demonstrates that younger, inexperienced, male, and minority members of a police force, who have little or no education, and perhaps prior military service have the highest degree of proactive behavior in terms of arrests and initiating citizen contacts, and thus can be considered at risk for problem behaviors. Conversely, being female, more experienced, more educated, etc. can be thought of as protective factors which can mitigate against problem behaviors. Additionally, although it is increasingly discussed in criminology, very little police research has considered the idea of protective factors, or events that might decrease the probability that an officer will engage in misconduct. Such factors might include job-related events like promotion (which presumably would carry with it less street time, and therefore less contact with citizens), skills training, and assignment to a quiet beat, or life events like marriage, having a child, etc. Such life events have been found to decrease the long-term (Sampson & Laub, 1990) and short-term (Horney et al., 1995) probability of criminal behavior for active offenders, so one might suspect such events to decrease the likelihood of misconduct for officers who experience such events. Some police-related protective factors found in the literature and thought to decrease the likelihood of misconduct may include: high educational attainment, a high level of job-related skill such as ability to communicate with others, and a positive occupational outlook.

One might also begin to think of police typologies with developmental considerations. As mentioned earlier, it is unclear from existing research if police types are sustainable over the course of an officer's career, or whether police might exhibit different operational styles at different points in their career. Additionally, one might take existing typologies and make some hypotheses about what the misconduct of an officer type looks like over time.

As an illustration, career misconduct pathways can be derived from Scrivner's (1994) five police profiles. Scrivner's first profile seems very similar to the conceptualization of the problem officer: they have an enduring, underlying trait (e.g., antisocial personality) that results in numerous problematic encounters with the public. Since the officer is not likely to learn from his/her mistakes, and the underlying cause is persistent, one would expect the officer's problem behavior to last a considerable length of time. As Scrivner notes, this is the group most highly at risk for excessive force, but is the smallest group she identifies.

If one were to apply criminal career terms to this profile, one would characterize these problem officers as those with an early onset (e.g., they begin their problematic behavior very early in their career), a high frequency (e.g., they would be involved in many incidents of problematic behavior compared to other officers), and a low probability of desistance, since their behavior is due to an enduring latent trait. One might also expect this officer to have a long duration, assuming no intervention by the police agency. However, such an assumption is obviously not viable as the most problematic officers are presumably the most at risk for receiving complaints, being involved in numerous use of force incidents, and having a civil case brought against them for their behavior. Since such acts will likely bring consequences from the police agency in the form of verbal reprimands by direct supervisors, suspensions, reassignment, or termination, one remains unsure as to the duration of problematic behavior for the problem officer since one is unsure of the deterrent impacts of these sanctions. However, there is no mention of problem officers being involved in corruption, so one might expect that while problem officers are subject to numerous disciplinary acts, their careers will not be immediately terminated like that of an officer caught engaging in acts of police corruption. The career length of problem officers, once identified, remains an empirical question.

Scrivner's second profile comes about because of excessive "emotional baggage" accumulated by an officer over their career course. Such officers suffer from burnout, which seems to peak at the intermediate career stage (6th to 15th year of policing) (Burke, 1989). One would expect such officers to exhibit a late onset in terms of problematic behavior, since it would take time to accumulate a critical mass of emotional baggage to result in problem behavior. When onset occurs, one might also expect frequency to be relatively high, especially when compared to other officers, but duration to be relatively short, since such uncharacteristic behavior would presumably get the attention of supervisors. In fact, one might view this uncharacteristic behavior and its subsequent intervention as a turning point, one that presumably would allow officers to acquire the assistance they need to deal with their emotional issues.

The third profile represents rookies who are eager, but not yet properly skilled through experience, and who often find themselves in problematic situations. One would expect such officers to have an early onset, since their problematic behavior is the result of inexperience, but a short duration, since their behavior should improve over time as their skill increases. These officers are likely to desist on their own after a few years on the job. The frequency of this group will be high during their relatively short stint in problem behavior when compared to other, more experienced officers. Note that this pattern is similar to the overall "experience-misconduct" curve posed earlier.

The fourth profile represents an officer whose problematic behavior stems from an inappropriate patrol style—a behavior learned on the job. One might suppose that this profile, over the course of one's career, would look very similar to the first profile. Indeed, both show a persistent problem that should result in multiple incidents of excessive force over the officer's career if left unchecked. However, the fourth profile begins their problematic behavior later in their career, since development of inappropriate patrol styles may take time. Also, since this profile lacks the number and severity of problematic precursors when compared to the first profile, one might expect fewer instances of problematic behavior. Put in criminal career terms, one would expect the fourth profile to have a somewhat later onset and a lower frequency than the first profile, but still possess a relatively longer duration than the second, third, or fifth profile.

The fifth profile discovered by Scrivner is the result of personal problem. Such officers' problematic behaviors tend to be episodic, with onset occurring at a time shortly after the start of the personal problem. The duration and frequency of problematic behavior will most likely vary with the duration and intensity of the problem, or with how well (or not) the officer manages to cope with the problem. Problems that appear later in an officer's career might produce a pattern indistinguishable from the pattern of the second profile, without some knowledge of what the officer is dealing with, be it burnout or some other personal issue.

What is interesting about Scrivner's profiles is that not only do they demonstrate varying degrees of onset, duration, and frequency, but they also display causes that include both state dependent and latent trait effects. For example, the first profile, the one that is congruent with the conceptualization of the problem officer, is caused by persistent antisocial traits, which manifest themselves in abusive tendencies. It is unlikely that such traits are on par with those of career criminals, since such individuals are highly unlikely to have steady employment or the educational attainment required for the police career. In fact, Scrivner mentions the traits possessed by an officer belonging to the first profile are not typically detected by the screening measures taken by police agencies, so presumably they are of a lower-order than those possessed by criminals with antisocial traits. However, the officers' traits become intensified with police work. Perhaps in another line of work, these antisocial traits would not cause problems for this person, but police officers must deal with people who are often belligerent, hostile, and rude. Such negative interactions would likely give an officer with antisocial traits more opportunity to manifest those traits, relative to other occupations. So for Scrivner, it is not simply the antisocial traits that cause police misconduct for problem officers; these traits must have opportunity to manifest themselves in situations that occur often in a police officer's line of work. One might go farther and suggest that if such officers are placed in areas where there is a high level of contact with citizens, their problems will be more readily apparent. Thus, one would expect an interaction between frequency of civilian contact and misconduct for these officer types. This is problematic, however, since one would expect a greater degree of misconduct generally (in the form of citizen complaints or uses of force) from officers assigned to high activity areas.

Scrivner's work is limited in that it only considers officers at risk for excessive force. While this is certainly a key problematic behavior and one that is most often discussed in conjunction with the problem officer, there are other forms of misconduct to consider as well. Verbal abuse, violation of a citizen's legal rights, failure to follow departmental guidelines, etc., are all examples of problematic behavior that is typically not covered in the discussion of problem officers. Expanding consideration of problem behavior beyond excessive force allows consideration of different career paths with different causes.

Besides just consideration of "offender" types, a developmental view of police behavior, if it is to parallel that of criminology, should also consider the "abstainer" type, or those officers who do not engage in misconduct. Some researchers in the criminological literature suggest that a certain amount of antisocial behavior is normative, and so perhaps a certain amount of police misconduct, particularly problem behaviors, should be expected given informal organizational norms described in the police literature. While few criminological studies have closely examined the non-offender population, they suggest that "abstainers" have problems of their own. For example Shedler and Block (1990), in a longitudinal analysis of drug experimentation of a sample of 130 males and females from the San Francisco area, found that while adolescents by age 18 who used drugs the most were the most maladjusted, those who had never used drugs were found to be relatively anxious, emotionally constricted, and lacking in social skills. Interestingly, those who had engaged in some drug experimentation were the best-adjusted teens in the sample.

Perhaps some degree of relatively minor police misconduct (e.g., discourtesy, failure to follow guidelines, etc.) is normative in the police world. After all, divided across hundreds or thousands of encounters, many involving citizens who are emotional or hostile, some discourtesy is probably a normal human response. As Moskos (2008) bluntly phrased it, "Like any other public employee with bad working conditions, obnoxious customers, and excellent job security, police get pissed off and can be assholes" (p. 10). It may be that those who engage in police misconduct often are seriously maladjusted to the police role, but those who never engage in police misconduct are, to some degree, maladjusted as well. While some might consider an officer with a perfect record of conduct to be the penultimate characterization of a professional, it would be interesting to know how this individual is considered among his/her fellow officers. Some research indicates that if an officer does not generate citizen complaints every so often, they will come under the suspicion of their immediate supervisors for avoiding police work (Lersch, 2002). There is also the added notion that police work itself cannot be fully brought under the rule of law (Bittner, 1970). Several police scholars have noted that the very nature of policing entails some degree of deviance in order to do the job (Bittner, 1970; Moskos, 2008; Skolnick & Fyfe, 1993); that all police officers at some time or another will violate the law or departmental policy is inevitable, which in fact may be encouraged in areas where laws or policies conflict with the reality of police work. Some of this deviance may be related to the administration of policing itself, given "that the role of police is best understood as a mechanism for the distribution of non-negotiably coercive force employed in the accordance with the dictates of an intuitive grasp of situational exigencies" (Bittner, 1970, p. 46). In short, police work is unique and is in many ways unlike any other profession, and some of its structural characteristics (e.g., little supervision, large amounts of discretion, etc.) can, one might argue, inevitably lead to deviance, despite a long history in policing of continuing—but failed—attempts to avoid or curtail it. Misconduct, under this view, is systemic to the occupation.

Finally, by adopting a developmental perspective of police behavior, one can consider the consequences of police misconduct. While some acts of police misconduct will certainly lead to career termination (and such events are worthy of study in their own right), others will not. It would be interesting to note the effects of misconduct on an officer. What happens when an officer receives his/her first citizen complaint? How long will it be until their next one? Officers can receive varying punishments for their misconduct in terms of verbal reprimands, official sanctions, forced leave, etc. Do these varying punishments have an effect on future misconduct? What is the probability of "recidivism" for these interventions? Criminology has benefited from consideration of the consequences of crime for an individual, and research on police misconduct can presumably benefit the same way. Criminology has found support for the idea that most criminals proceed along a series of behavioral sequences in their criminal careers, and it would be interesting to note if police misconduct proceeds in a similar matter. Some researchers like Sherman (1974) have suggested such a process in explaining police graft and police burglary, and there are hints in the socialization literature that excessive force might follow a sequence as well, and these are the types of developmental processes police researchers should consider in future research.

Overall, thinking about police misconduct in terms of a developmental framework has several advantages over other ways of considering this behavior. By focusing on individuals over time, instead of comparing individuals to each other, researchers get further at the idea of causality (specifically by parceling out time ordering). Moreover, by couching police behavior in developmental terms, one can begin to consider how life events (including the act of misconduct itself) have effects on misconduct's onset, frequency, duration, and desistance. By considering causal factors and how they might impact a career, one can think about both proximal (e.g., a change in assignment) and more enduring (e.g., antisocial traits possessed by an officer) causes of misconduct, and how the two might even interact over the course of an officer's career (see, for example, Toch, 1996). While some research along these lines has already been done, it can now be brought under the umbrella of a developmental framework and enhanced by its consideration.

Touting the advantages of a developmental view of police misconduct is not meant to imply that it can circumvent the problems of measurement and evidence which plagues research in this area. Far from it. Misconduct will always be difficult to measure empirically, and thus all work in this area will tend to focus on less serious acts. But work in police misconduct can certainly gain from consideration of the criminal career paradigm and life-course criminology more generally, through an adoption and adaptation of a developmental framework in terms of a police career.

Conclusion

The early experiences of officers can shape their future behaviors, and officers' level of experience can impact how they behave, especially with regard to their level of misconduct. Based on the police literature, the existence of a police "experience-misconduct" curve is posed, thus necessitating consideration as to whether there may exist differing career misconduct paths underlying this aggregate curve. The research on police typologies and the problem officer, combined with what scholars know already from the criminological literature, proposes the existence of: (1) a group of persistent, problematic officers who engages in misconduct throughout the course of their career, (2) a group of officers who follow the aggregate "experience-misconduct" curve, and by implication (3) an "abstainer" group, or those who never engages in misconduct, or who do so at extremely low levels. Other career misconduct paths may exist, but evidence to support such hypotheses from the policing literature is weak at best. A contribution to policing literature would be to examine the misconduct of officers over a large section of their career course, and to discover if there exist any distinct career paths within the police population. Moreover, since such a contribution would be largely exploratory, it would be enlightening to apply the criminal career constructs of participation, onset, length, frequency, and desistance in terms of police misconduct as well attempt to simply describe patterns of this behavior over an officer's career, since no such research exists on this topic.

Such analyses would contribute to policing in much the same way as similar analyses have contributed in criminology. First, knowledge of developmental pathways can help to pinpoint more accurately the warning signs that indicate deviation from normal development. Specifically, we can discover what level of misconduct is typical of officers, and how and when other officers deviate from the normal pattern. Second, such analyses would also provide knowledge about when to specifically target interventions.

For example, if there is a place in officers' careers where misconduct spikes, this suggests a critical period in which influential processes operate that facilitate that increase, directing researchers to more closely examine proximal causal mechanisms or risk factors that prompted the behavior. Third, these analyses will tell us something about the probability that misconduct will be maintained over the career course, since the results of cross sectional research leaves the concept of a problem officer who engages in deviance throughout his/her career course in doubt.

Chapter 3

The Early Intervention System Project

In the previous chapter, a number of hypotheses were posed about the patterns of police misconduct over the course of officers' careers. It was noted that early work on police implied a single underlying pattern of police misconduct over time, assuming that all officers are shaped by the socialization process in more-or-less the same way. Other police researchers though wondered whether police officers develop distinctive ways for dealing with the challenges associated with their work, leading to a suspicion that patterns of problem behaviors may be different depending on the officer(s) under consideration.

This chapter considers these two different explanations of police misconduct by describing a series of analyses designed to test whether there is a single, or multiple, patterns of police misconduct over time. Discussion begins with the core research questions to be addressed in the remainder of this book, and the data and analytic plan utilized in answering them.

Research Questions and Related Objectives

The first research question deals with misconduct over time: is there a relationship between experience and misconduct in the aggregate? If so, what does it look like and tell us about misconduct? The implication of an aggregate experience-misconduct curve was noted earlier, and thus it would prove useful to more closely examine aggregate misconduct patterns. The research on problem officers suggests that misconduct will be most often confined to a small group of officers, implying that the incidence (i.e., frequency) of misconduct is of greater concern than its prevalence (i.e., participation). Yet all research on problem behaviors to date has been cross-sectional and has not explicitly examined career dimensions, so the relationship of incidence to prevalence over officer careers remains an empirical question, as do other features such as onset, duration, and desistance.

The second and related question concerns the existence of varying trajectories of officer misconduct which may underlie an aggregate curve. Recall that in the criminal career literature, Nagin and Land (1993) found that while offending at the individual level was single-peaked, much like the aggregate age-crime curve, individuals differed in their offending over age. While some offenders followed a trajectory over time that looked much like the aggregate age-crime curve, the authors also found evidence of two additional trajectories that deviated from the aggregate curve. In a similar vein, one might reasonably expect that different officer trajectories may underlie an aggregate curve describing the relationship between experience and misconduct. Chapter 2 specified what trajectories one might expect given extant police research, but the actual number and patterns of these trajectories have never been explored, and thus also remains an empirical question worthy of investigation.

From these two research questions follows three general objectives which shapes the analyses to be conducted, and whose results are to be described in subsequent chapters. First, careers of police misconduct in the aggregate are described, including the shape of the experience-misconduct curve and the five elements of misconduct careers: participation, onset, desistance, frequency, and duration. Second, police misconduct careers are disaggregated to determine whether subgroups of officers follow different career trajectories. The semiparametric, group-based approach developed by Nagin (1999; 2005) is employed here to examine trajectories of police misconduct. This procedure allows one to discover if there are multiple trajectories of police misconduct over the course of policing careers, and the specific behavior patterns of those trajectories. The third and related objective is to examine the risk factors, protective factors, and correlates of different trajectories. It was noted previously that some officer characteristics such as race, sex, education, and military experience may be risk or protective factors for problem behaviors. Since the subject officers can be sorted into their respective misconduct trajectories, a profile of each trajectory can be constructed, thus examining whether demographic and background characteristics are associated with a given career path. In addition, one can examine if other behaviors, such as arrest productivity, uses of force, and involvement in civil litigation are related to these trajectories in expected ways.

Data Collection

The data to be employed here were collected as part of an Early Intervention System (EIS) project for a large police department in the northeastern United States.[1] An EIS is a behavior-management tool used for identifying potential problematic officers, and includes selection criteria by which officers are selected for intervention. Most utilize various indicators of problematic police performance such as personnel complaints, involvement in civil litigation, use of force reports, etc to identify officers whose patterns of performance warrant intervention. Most of these systems also provide for numerical thresholds of specified events over a specific time frame (e.g., 3 citizen complaints in a six-month period). But the validity of the implicit predictions on which these systems are

---

1. As part of the agreement between the research team and the police agency under study, the agency can only be referred to in these terms, and no additional identifying characteristics can be provided.

based has not been established by research; researchers do not know if officers selected based on any given criteria will display a continued pattern of problematic behavior in the absence of an intervention. Thus, the primary purpose of this research project was to form the foundation of an EIS based on careful assessment of the advantages and disadvantages of alternative selection criteria. The research presented here is a secondary analysis of these data, which are ideal because they contain indicators of problematic police performance over the course of officer careers.

Generally, these data contain several indicators of police behavior for all sworn officers who were employed by this police agency from January 1st, 1987 through June 30th, 2001. There are certain exceptions to this, however, and they will be noted in the discussion of the various indicators. The sampled timeframe was decided upon mainly by how far back the agency kept computerized records of various behavioral indicators. In addition, there are data on officers' demographic characteristics (race, and sex), as well as data on various officers' background characteristics (education and prior military experience).

The data were retrieved from various administrative offices at agency headquarters beginning in late 2001 and continuing through late 2002 by the research team, which included a sergeant who served as liaison to the clerical personnel responsible for maintaining these data. The team encountered little problem in obtaining the data, since it was widely known that agency leadership approved of this project, and moreover, considered it a priority. Once retrieved, each database was checked for omissions and errors, and the research team searched additional electronic and paper records in an attempt to fix these problems when necessary.

Cohorts

To maximize the advantages of when these data were obtained, officers who entered the police agency during the study period were selected and placed into cohorts. Two cohorts are selected based on each officer's date of entry. The first, who are termed the Late 1980s cohort, consists of officers who entered the agency between January 1st, 1987 and December 31st, 1990. These officers, by the end of the sample period, have the potential to serve 11.5 to 14.5 years, although some officers will certainly leave the agency before this period. The second cohort, who I call the Early 1990s cohort, consists of officer who entered the agency between January 1st, 1991 and December 31st 1994. These officers, by the end of the sample period, have the potential to serve 7.5 to 10.5 years, and again, some may leave before this period. Table 3.1 lists the number of officers who reside in their respective cohorts based on year of entry.

Table 3.1 Cohort Populations by Year of Entry

Year of Entry	Late 1980s Cohort	Early 1990s Cohort
1987	483	—
1988	385	—
1989	283	—
1990	276	—
1991	—	51
1992	—	240
1993	—	99
1994	—	328
	N = 1427	N = 718

The Late 1980s cohort has 1,427 officers, and is fairly evenly distributed based on year of entry, although the number of officers does decrease across the study period. The Early 1990s cohort has 718 officers, and the number of officers hired in each year varies considerably across year of entry. Both of these cohorts have an adequate number of cases to conduct the analyses presented below.

Attrition

Since this is a retrospective, longitudinal study, attrition from the police force can be an issue, especially if officers in each cohort tend not to serve the majority of the years for which the EIS project obtained information. Table 3.2 presents information on attrition by cohort. From this table, one can observe that more than seventy percent of the officers in both cohorts served from their date of entry through the entire remaining observation period. Of those who did not, the vast majority were officers who served less than one year, and in fact most of these were officers who never made it out of the training academy. The remaining officers who did not serve for the entire observation period were randomly scattered across years of experience, with no more than 18 officers leaving in any particular year in the Late 1980s cohort, and no more than 27 officers leaving in any particular year in the Early 1990s cohort.

Table 3.2 Attrition Information

	Late 1980s Cohort	Early 1990s Cohort
Career Data		
Officers who served entire period (%)	70.2	76.2
Officers who did not serve entire period (%)	29.8	23.8
Total (%)	100.0	100.0
N =	1427	718
Officers who left		
Officers who left serving less than 1 year (%)	68.0	61.4
Officers who left serving more than 1 year (%)	32.0	38.6
Total (%)	100.0	100.0
N =	425	171

The officers who left with less than one year of experience are significantly different within each cohort both in terms of their background and demographic characteristics than those who remained, and thus are excluded from subsequent analyses.[2]

The demographic and background characteristics of these cohorts are described in Table 3.3. There are some important differ-

Table 3.3 Demographic and Background Characteristics

	Late 1980s Cohort	Early 1990s Cohort
Gender		
Male (%)	90.3	86.5
Female (%)	9.7	13.5
Total	100.0	100.0
Race		
White (%)	73.2	82.9
Black (%)	16.0	9.0
Hispanic (%)	10.3	7.6
Other (%)	0.5	0.5
Total	100.0	100.0
Background Characteristics		
Military Service (%)	8.2	14.4
No Military Service (%)	91.8	85.6
Total	100.0	100.0
Degree (%)	48.3	70.5
No Degree (%)	51.7	29.5
Total	100.0	100.0
Mean Age of Entry	24.5	25.6
n =	1138	613

2. Officers who served more than one year, but left before the study period ended were generally not significantly different in terms of their demographic and background characteristics than the rest of their respective cohorts. A few significant differences did emerge, but their actual differences were very small, and it is suspected that differences emerged due to large sample sizes and are not substantively important.

ences between the cohorts. The Early 1990s cohort contains more females than the Late 1980s cohort, even though the vast majority of the officers are male, and less than one-tenth of the officers are female. The racial makeup of these cohorts differs, with a greater percentage of the Late 1980s cohort being Black or Hispanic when compared to the Early 1990s cohort. There was a large effort on the part of the police agency to hire more minority candidates during the 1980s, which may account for the greater number of Blacks and Hispanics in this time period. The education levels of the officers also differ, with the Early 1990s cohort officers being more likely to have a college degree when compared to the Late 1990s cohort. This reflects a demographic shift in the applicant pool characteristic of the larger population who are increasingly likely to be college educated. The Early 1990s cohort was also much more likely to have officers with prior military service when compared to the Late 1980s cohort. The mean age at entry was different for the two cohorts as well, with the Early 1990s cohort entering about a year later on average than the Late 1980s cohort. All of the differences in both demographic and background characteristics between the cohorts were statistically significant based on Chi-Square tests.

The current cohort strategy has several advantages. First, it minimizes cohort effects. All 7,130 officers who served this police agency during the study period are at various career stages: some officers served while in the middle of their careers, some retired during the sampled timeframe, and others had just begun. To minimize the possible confound that officers entering this agency in different decades may differ in significant ways from each other, only officers entering in 1987–1994 are examined. Second, some interest lies in deciding if problem officers are problematic across their career or are actually just "gung ho" rookie officers, so it makes sense to focus upon the early-to-mid stages of an officer's career, which can be accomplished with these cohorts. No study on problem officers or police misconduct has examined more than 5 years worth of data, and these were cross sectional studies. Utilizing the current strategy, officers in two cohorts are examined, instead of comparing officers at varying points in their careers from different time periods.

While the modal career length for officers in this agency is presumably 20 years, since this is the time at which officers can retire with their full pension, this strategy can examine a subset of officers who have served over a quarter to half of their career term. Third, by using two cohorts, comparisons of the stability of the findings across years of experience, with each cohort serving as a comparison group to the other, can be made.[3]

Variables

The variables collected for the EIS Project and to be utilized in the following chapters are listed in Table 3.4. The table specifies each concept and the indicator to which it is tied, as well as the time period for which the indicator could be obtained by the research team.

Indicators of Misconduct
Personnel Complaints

The key dependent variables representing problem behaviors in this study are personnel complaints. Data on personnel complaints include both complaints by citizens as well as internally-generated complaints. The database that includes this information is maintained by the agency's Internal Affair Bureau, and contains fields for the date of the incident, the source of the complaint (citizen or po-

---

3. There were no significant period effects (e.g., changes in training, etc.) that could be identified which would make the cohorts incomparable. The agency hired no officers in 1995, so the preceding years from 1987–1994 were simply divided in half. One could argue each academy class is different, with different instructors, instructor-to-student ratios, etc., but considering each class individually would not produce enough cases for analysis.

Table 3.4 Concepts & Indicators

Dependent Variables

Citizen Complaints: collected for January 1st, 1987–June 30th, 2001

Internal Complaints: collected for January 1st, 1987–June 30th, 2001

Risk Factors, Protective Factors, & Correlates

Demographic characteristics: collected for January 1st, 1987–June 30th, 2001

    Race of officer: White, Black, Hispanic, Other

    Sex of officer: Male, Female

Background characteristics: collected January 1st, 1987–June 30th, 2001

    Prior military experience: Yes / No

    College degree earned by June 30th, 2001: Yes / No

Uses of Force: collected for January 1st, 1995–June 30th, 2001

Civil Litigation: collected for January 1st, 1991–June 30th, 2001

Secondary Arrests: collected for January 1st, 1987–June 30th, 2001 (sample)

Control Variables

Sick leave usage: collected for January 1st, 1991–June 30th, 2001

Date of first rank: collected for January 1st, 1987–June 30th, 2001

Penal law arrests: collected for January 1st, 1987–December 31st, 2000 (sample)

---

lice), the nature of the allegations, and the complaint's disposition. These data encompass the entire study period: January 1st, 1987 to June 30th, 2001.

Citizen Complaints

The agency that is the host of this research takes citizen complaints in person, by mail, by phone, by fax, and via e-mail from the agency's website. There is, at least officially, no authorized discretion in the taking of citizen complaints. Any citizen complaint made is to be recorded, and forwarded to the appropriate personnel for investigation. Since this agency takes citizen complaints by phone and in person at its various stations, this gives the personnel in these stations some control over complaints at intake. One might suppose that some citizen complaints are handled informally, with a supervisor (such as a sergeant) listening to a complainant and promising an officer will be "spoken to," but no formal complaint is registered with the agency. This may not necessarily be a negative experience for citizens, who might leave satisfied that someone heard their grievance, and that the officer in question will come under some supervisory scrutiny. In terms of capturing these complaints in official records, however, such informal handling of complaints reduces the number of citizen complaints any given officer is likely to have on his or her record.

At the same time, this agency takes complaints anonymously, and does not require the citizen to sign a complaint document. As long as the citizen provides enough information about the incident (the location, date, time, etc.) so that an officer can be properly identified, an investigation into the allegation will occur (so the citizen is not required to know the officer's name). Some police agencies, especially those that control the complaint process, have been known to require citizens to sign legal documents stating that their complaint is valid, and if it is found not to be so, the citizen can be the subject of legal action for registering a false complaint (Caiden & Hahn, 1979). The agency under investigation here does not have this requirement. These two factors, taking anonymous complaints and not requiring citizens to sign a legal document, makes the complaint process less burdensome to citizens, and makes citizen complaints more likely when compared to agencies that do not take complaints anonymously and require citizens to sign a legal document.

In the analyses of citizen complaints, all such complaints filed against officers are utilized. An alternative strategy would be to use only those citizen complaints where the facts substantiate the specific allegation(s) of misconduct. However, such a strategy is limiting as previous research demonstrates that in the vast majority of cases, the only person witnessing an alleged act of misconduct is the complainant. Such cases become "swearing contests" in which the officer and citizen allege their version of events is true, with these cases resulting in a complaint being unsubstantiated (i.e., there is no way to prove or disprove the allegation). Moreover, since most cases are unsubstantiated, limiting analyses to only substantiated complaints reduces the already infrequent cases of citizen complaints even further, reducing the chances for meaningful quantitative analyses. More importantly, it would leave one with even more severe misconduct, as cases that were substantiated presumably would be the most serious.

One might also be interested in specific types of citizen complaints, since some problem officer research has limited complaint types to specific problems such as excessive force, discourtesy, etc. The data do provide information on complaint types, of which there are over fifty, but these were devised and categorized by the person responsible for maintaining these data, and as such do not contain definitions or criteria by which these types are determined. The agency at the time of the study was working on developing specific complaint types and developing procedures to categorize them, and as such it is suspected that the present categories lack validity. For those interested, just over half of all citizen complaints in each cohort were accounted for by five categories: (1) improper police action (14.5%), (2) unprofessional conduct (10.8%), (3) excessive force (9.2%), (4) negligence (8.9%), and (5) service (8.9%), but again, these are not well defined. None of the remaining categories accounted for more than 4 percent of the citizen complaints filed, and most account for 1 percent or less. The analyses reported herein consider all citizen complaint types. This does capture a wide variation of behaviors which range in severity, but given the questionable validity of the complaint categories, this seems the best course of action. In analyses of citizen complaint trajectories, a subset of complaints were used that appeared to best match the traditional problem officer concept was employed, but this did not serve to better locate a problem officer trajectory, and only decreased the power of the overall model. More discussion of this follows in Chapter 5.

Internal Complaints

Internally-generated complaints filed against officers are also an important misconduct indicator. These complaints are filed by other officers, either peers or supervisors, but follow the same procedures as citizen complaints. These complaints presumably avoid some of the pitfalls of using citizen complaints, since officers have frequent contact with each other and understand what is and is not acceptable according to policy. However, these complaints may also be handled informally, as one officer may simply express concern to another officer's supervisor and may not wish to file a formal complaint internally. As with citizen complaints, all internal complaints are employed, regardless of type or disposition. The choice to use these complaints without considering disposition is less troublesome for internal complaints, as only five percent of these complaints were unsubstantiated. This is in line with other research which demonstrates a much larger percentage of substantiated dispositions for internal complaints when compared with citizen complaints (Griswold, 1990; Liederbach et al., 2007).

Independent Variables

The key independent variable in this research is the year of experience for each officer. Years of experience were calculated based on an officer's date of entry, and each complaint was placed into a year of experience based on the date in which it was filed.[4] Thus, for each officer, the officer-complaint file tallies the total number of complaints for each year of experience until the observation period ended or the officer left the agency.[5]

---

4. Some complaints were missing a filing date, so it was estimated based on the ordinary time lag between receipt of a complaint and the date that reports are either due or are received.

5. Information was available on the date when all officers left this agency, and as such the data can distinguish between observation periods

The other independent variables, thought to impact the risk for misconduct, comprise the demographic characteristics of officers such as race, coded as White, Black, Hispanic, and Other (either Asian or Native American); sex, coded as Male or Female; and the dichotomous background characteristics regarding prior military experience [Yes/No] and attainment of a college degree [Yes/No], which means an Associates degree or higher. This information was retrieved for each officer from the personnel data system at the agency headquarters.

Correlates of Misconduct

Use of Force

There are other correlates of misconduct, or indicators whose relationship to misconduct can be examined, captured in the dataset. The first correlate is use of force. Data on uses of force are also maintained by the Internal Affairs Bureau and encompass incidents in which either an officer or a citizen is injured (or claims injury), or in which OC pepper spray or some other instrument (e.g., a baton) is used. This database contains information on the date of the incident, the officers involved, and the form of force that was used. This particular database contains information for a shorter duration than personnel complaints: from January 1st, 1995 to June 30th, 2001.

According to departmental policy, anytime an officer is injured or is thought to have caused an injury to a citizen, no matter how slight (this includes simple complaining of any pain), the officer must report this injury to a sergeant who conducts an investigation.[6] The sergeant then provides a memorandum in the form of an administrative teletype sent from the station to headquarters, which

---

where an officer received zero citizen complaints and observation periods after an officer left the agency.

6. The use of OC pepper spray is to be reported, but is not the subject of an investigation.

includes statements from the officer, the injured party, and any witnesses to the event containing the sum and substance of what occurred. The information from the teletype is entered into a database by clerical personnel working at headquarters. This database has only recently taken computerized form, which is why the research team could only obtain records dating back to 1995. Presumably this indicator is reliable, given that officers must record their injuries in case they require leave or workers compensation, and are also very likely to record citizen injuries in case of a later complaint or civil litigation (officers have great incentive to "cover their ass"). It is hypothesized that officers with high rates of citizen complaints also have high rates of uses of force, even though effective police work necessitates that officers use force on occasion.

Civil Litigation

Another correlate is involvement in civil litigation. Data on involvement in civil litigation measures incidents in which a citizen brings forth legal action against an officer. This database is maintained by the agency's Legal Department and contains information on the officers involved, the nature of the allegation, the date the legal action occurred, and the trial disposition. While data have been obtained for the entire study period, it appears that the database is incomplete before 1992. As such, only the information contained in the civil litigation database after the 1991 calendar year will be employed here. It is hypothesized that officers with high rates of citizen complaints will also be at an increased risk of civil litigation.

Secondary Arrests

The third correlate of misconduct is secondary arrests. This indicator is a subset of all the penal law arrests made by a sample of the officers, which is described below, and is commonly thought to point to problems occurring within the police-citizen encounter. These arrest charges are in addition to the primary arrest charge, and include charges such as resisting arrest, assault on a police officer, harassment, escape from custody, etc.[7] As mentioned previously, research has indicated that officers who violate official rules in police-citizen encounters sometimes arrest potential complainants, knowing that persons charged with crimes are given less standing than those who are not (Bittner, 1970; Chevigny, 1969). It is hypothesized that officers with high rates of citizen complaints will also have higher secondary arrest rates, even though routine police work may necessitate that officers use these arrest charges.

The agency's Information Services department maintains the data on arrests. Each time a penal law arrest is made, the information is entered into a department-wide database. The arrest database contains information on the arresting officer (e.g., name, shield number, etc.), the date of arrest, and the charges filed. The arrest data are available for the entire study period.

The research team confronted a complication with the arrest variable. To acquire all penal law arrests (both primary and secondary) made by each officer during the study period would have been a tremendous undertaking, as these data were maintained on an archaic computer system in the agency's Information Services department. Only one individual in the department knew how to extract the arrest data, and so to alleviate the burden on this person and obtain the data in a timely fashion for project completion, a sample of officers was selected. The research team selected entire academy sessions for sampling. All officers who entered in 1987, 1992, 1994 and 1996 were selected and arrest data were obtained for these officers. This works well for present purposes, given that all but the officers in 1996 fit into the cohorts.

The number of officers for whom arrest data were obtained is listed by cohort in Table 3.5. For the entire study period, the EIS project obtained arrest data on 1,800 officers, or about one-quarter of the entire population. When the officers selected in 1996 are removed because they fit into neither cohort, the number drops to 1,150 of-

---

7. These charges were decided upon from input from the agency's command staff.

Table 3.5 Arrest Data Availability

Cohort	Officers with Arrest Data	Officers without Arrest Data
Late 1980s	278	1149
Early 1990s	361	357
	n = 639	n = 1506

ficers, or 16 percent of the population. Table 3.5, demonstrates that arrest data was obtained for about 20 percent of the officers in the late 1980s cohort and about 50 percent of the officers in the late 1990s cohort. The officers who have arrest data do not vary significantly in their demographic and background characteristics from the rest of the officers from their respective cohorts.

Control Variables

Sick Leave

There are a number of variables which, if not considered, might bias the analyses in the remaining chapters. The first control variable to consider is sick leave usage. The database on sick leave usage is maintained by the agency's Office of Human Resources and includes the date of the leave, the type of leave used, and the number of hours used. Theses data are reported reliably only beginning in 1991, so the information includes sick leave usage of all officers from January 1st, 1991 to June 30th, 2001. The primary purpose of utilizing this indicator is to control for exposure time, so interest lies in the dates of sick leave, and the amount of work hours missed. Officers out on sick leave are not subject to personnel complaints, uses of force, and the like, so it is necessary to consider when officers are on the street. However, since data is available for the Early 1990s cohort, it will only be utilized for this group. Since most officers used no sick leave, or if sick leave was used, very few days were taken, the results for the Early 1990s cohort are virtually identical when employing sick leave usage as a consideration when generating results. Thus, the results presented in the subsequent chapters does not control for sick leave.

Assignment

The second control variable to examine is the officer's assignment, particularly whether to consider only when officers were serving in patrol, or to consider times when officers were also promoted to either investigative or supervisory functions. One can reasonably assume that officers above the rank of patrol are less at-risk for personnel complaints. The data for the EIS project contain dates upon which an officer was first promoted and support this contention: nearly four-fifths of all personnel complaints are filed against patrol officers. However, limiting the analyses to patrol officers would presumably truncate the careers of officers least likely to generate complaints, since the skilled officers are presumably the ones who are promoted the fastest, and might therefore bias the analyses. As such, all analyses reported herein differentiate between considering all officers regardless of rank, and analyses which consider only times when officers were assigned to patrol. In the aggregate analyses, consideration of rank does at times make a difference, and so different series of analyses are undertaken. In the trajectory analyses, consideration of rank had almost no bearing on the results, and made no difference in the substantive conclusions drawn from them, and so analyses consider all officers regardless of rank.

The other consideration of officer assignment is the actual location where officers are assigned. One might suspect that certain assignments carry with them higher work loads, and hence would impact the frequency with which officers have contact with citizens. All else being equal, officers who have busier assignments will have more contact with the public, and therefore would be a greater risk for citizen complaints. Moreover, some assignments might contain more complaint-prone citizens, which have to do with the nature and history of police-citizen relationships in varying locations.

The agency under study does not track officers' assignments across their career, and so data is only available on officers' current assignment. Assignment is recorded in the complaint data, but this does not provide a clear picture of officers' assignment histories, except possibly for those officers with a large number of complaints. The agency under study does rotate officer shifts regardless of seniority, and as such experience does not allow officers to only work days or nights. Actual assignments, however, are based on a bidding system, of which seniority is a considering factor, and so one might suspect that the younger officers are assigned to the most active areas. This agency though, as mentioned at the outset, is rather large, and thus has a correspondingly large number of assignments. This limits the generalizability of the findings to other agencies, but also minimizes the likelihood that only a few assignments are disproportionately responsible for the number of complaints officers receive due to workload or other factors unrelated to a proclivity for misconduct.

With regards to the certain assignments containing more complaint-prone citizens, the EIS team conducted analyses using all officers in the sample timeframe and their last assignment, and found that no one assignment stood out as more complaint-prone than any other. This was surprising, and there was nearly as much variation *within* assignments than there were *between* them. This appear to indicate that as a unit of analysis, assignments have considerable variation in terms of complaints filed, which likely reflects the variation in officers' propensities for problem behaviors within them, more so than other factors such as shift (day/night), workload, or the characteristics of citizens who reside in certain assignment locations.

Productivity

The third control variable is productivity, which to some extent takes into consideration the workload of officers' varying assignments over their career. Recall from Chapter 2 that some police scholars have theorized that the best officers are the ones engaging in proactive police activity, and will therefore be the subject of more citizen complaints when compared to less active officers, regardless of their actual misconduct levels. In short this "good apples" hypothesis (Lersch, 2002) states that citizen complaints are better measures of productivity than of police deviance. Productivity is measured here by the frequency of penal law arrests made over the course of an officer's career. Again, data for all of the cohort officers for this indicator is unavailable. The sample of officers who do have these data will be utilized to determine if officers who engage in greater arrest productivity will also be the most likely to be the subject of citizen complaints.

Analyses

There are generally two series of analyses to be conducted here, and are presented in the proceeding chapters. The first set of analyses aims to examine the aggregate pattern of personnel complaints and their related career dimensions of onset, duration, frequency, desistance, and participation. These are presented in Chapter 4. The second set of analyses aims to disaggregate misconduct careers, for both citizen and internal complaints, into different patterns over time, and sort officers into their respective career paths. Once accomplished, the relationship of these career paths to other correlates can be examined, and trajectory profiles based on demographic and background characteristics can be constructed. The analyses based upon citizen complaints are presented in Chapter 5, and analyses based upon internal complaints are presented in Chapter 6.

Conclusion

Police misconduct can have potentially devastating impacts on the police organization and its relationship with the public. The notion that a small group of problem officers may account for a disproportionate amount of misconduct offers administrators a more specific population on which to target scarce intervention resources, but more research is required to: (a) identify who these officers are, (b) discover what characteristics these officers have in common, and (c) attempt to find out why these officers are the subject of so many complaints.

The previous literature on problem officers has attempted to identify these officers by their background characteristics, some while controlling the officer's assignment and arrest activity, and notes that the younger, inexperienced, male officers are most likely to be problems. But the concept of a problem officer implicitly assumes that these officers are problematic throughout their career, at least until they are either terminated or the subject of some intervention. So the question remains, are the young problem officers just active rookies who will mature out of their problematic behaviors, or might there be different problem officer types?

To answer such a question, one requires data of sufficient length so as to identify problem officers and follow the course of their careers in misconduct. By determining if different career paths exist, one can determine if the typical characterization of the problem officer is valid, or whether there might be other distinct types of misconduct trajectories. Moreover, by developing general profiles of different trajectories, one can know what type of officers are most at-risk for developing specific patterns of problematic behavior.

What might this mean for policy? First, for devising alternative or new strategies to combat misconduct, one needs to consider the relative contributions of both participation and frequency. If, for example, misconduct is widespread throughout the officer population (e.g., high participation), with many officers being only sporadically problematic, then participation is an appropriate target for misconduct intervention. Alternatively, if participation is low and individual frequency rates are high for a small group of officers, then policies directed at these high-rate officers may be more suitable. Moreover, if one finds that some officers are high-rate officers, but only at certain career points, this also suggests targeting these officers, but perhaps with differing intervention strategies. For example, a finding that young, male officers are problematic in their first 3 to 4 years of experience, but tend to desist thereafter, suggests a different intervention strategy than officers who are frequently problematic for a short period of time in the middle or later part of their career.

Also, by knowing what types of officers are more predisposed to which kinds of career misconduct patterns, administrators can know which patterns are most likely to be prevalent in their organization based on its demographic makeup. Additionally, although officers' demographic characteristics may not be directly manipulated in an organizational setting, the traits identified as being conducive to a certain trajectory can serve as a basis for selection decisions. For example, police departments nationwide are encouraging officers to become college educated under the theory that they are better performers. If it is found that college educated officers are most likely to be in the abstainer (i.e., non offender) trajectory, this would help substantiate those claims. Similarly, many departments are actively recruiting female candidates under the hypothesis that female officers interact better with citizens than male officers, and are less likely to resort to using force. To the extent that female officers are less likely to be assigned to a misconduct trajectory, be involved in citizen complaints, or use force, the results of this analysis might also help substantiate these claims.

While these analyses can identify the problem officers, and can even account for multiple groups of problem officers, and can also discover the characteristics these officers have in common, these analyses cannot address the last question posed above: to discover why problem officers receive so many complaints or rate high on other misconduct indicators. The timing and frequency of citizen and internal complaints against an officer can be examined, and which characteristics might predispose an officer to a certain career pattern of misconduct can be uncovered, but these data cannot ultimately explain why some officers receive a high frequency of complaints. It will be impossible to say why some officers, for example, may be episodically problematic, while others are enduringly problematic, and why some never are involved in misconduct at all (net of measurement error).

Still, this research is a necessary first-step in determining both aggregate patterns of misconduct and individual career paths. Both sets of analyses will tell police scholars something about the misconduct careers of officers, which can lead to more informed policy decisions which target this important police issue.

Chapter 4

The Experience-Misconduct Curves

The first hypothesis to be tested is whether at the aggregate level there exists an experience-misconduct curve. The literature on police misconduct seems to suggest that officers will tend to get into trouble early in their career, and so misconduct, as measured by personnel complaints, will peak in the first few years of experience, but will then steadily decline thereafter. The reasons for this decline are varied: it may be that officers mature, gain in skill, obtain greater stakes in conformity, and as van Maanen (1973) suggests, are encouraged to "lay low and avoid trouble." Another hypothesis may be that officers do not necessarily perform better during encounters with citizens, but instead simply become better at avoiding complaints, or situations where citizens are more likely *to* complain. Whichever explanation is correct, there is support for the hypothesis of an experience-misconduct curve in these data. The aggregate curves for the Late 1980s and Early 1990s cohorts are presented in Figures 4.1 and 4.2 respectively.[1]

When examining these figures, it is apparent that experience and misconduct are related in an orderly way at the aggregate level. Both figures show a peak in misconduct early in officers' careers, al-

---

1. One might suspect that each academy class is different, and hence these curves mask interesting variation in the relationship between experience and misconduct. While the average number of complaints and the years that each academy class peaks varies, the conclusions derived from observing these curves by cohort or by academy class are not substantively different.

Figure 4.1 Average Personnel Complaints by Year of
Experience for Late 1980s Cohort

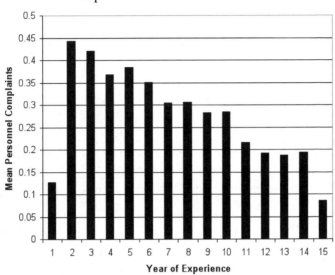

Figure 4.2 Average Personnel Complaints by Year of
Experience for Early 1990s Cohort

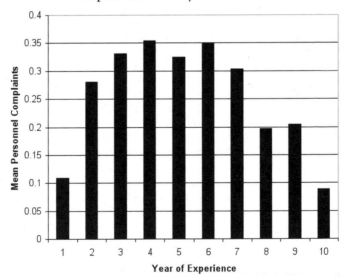

though the peak is somewhat different between the cohorts. The Late 1980s cohort shows a sharp peak in average personnel complaints in years two and three, with a steady decline thereafter, while the Early 1990s cohort shows a steadier rise in years one to three, a peak in years four to six, and a steady decline thereafter. The sharp increase between the first and second year of experience is likely due to the six months of academy training officers attend during their first year. Even though a few officers managed to have citizen complaints filed against them while in the academy, their exposure to the public is limited and therefore complaints unlikely. Also, the drop in the last year of experience is due to only six months of data collected for 2001.

One must also consider the aggregate pattern of both citizen complaints and internal complaints. Given that the majority of complaints filed against officers are citizen complaints, one would expect that the aggregate curve of this complaint type would match that of the personnel complaint pattern. Internal complaints, however, might not necessarily follow this pattern, since very few of them are filed, and research has yet to examine them exclusively.

Figures 4.3 and 4.4 present the experience-misconduct curves for their respective cohorts using only citizen complaints for all officers. As expected, the patterns of citizen complaints are very similar to the pattern of personnel complaints for the respective cohorts: there is a peak in the early years of experience with a steady decline thereafter. The citizen complaint curves for patrol officers only for both cohorts (not presented) match that of citizen complaints when considering all officers, except that the latter half of the distribution displays slightly higher averages, since patrol officers are at a greater risk for citizen complaints. Still, the patterns when considering all officers or just patrol officers are virtually indistinguishable.

Figures 4.5 and 4.6 present the experience-misconduct curves for the two cohorts using only internal complaints for all officers.[2]

2. There were no internal complaints filed against officers in the Early 1990s cohort for the first 6 months of 2001.

Figure 4.3 Average Citizen Complaints by Year of
Experience for Late 1980s Cohort

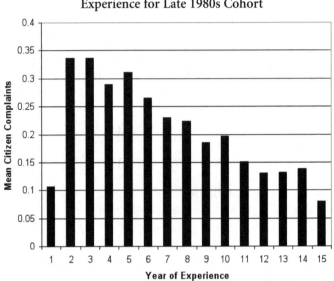

Figure 4.4 Average Citizen Complaints by Year of
Experience for Early 1990s Cohort

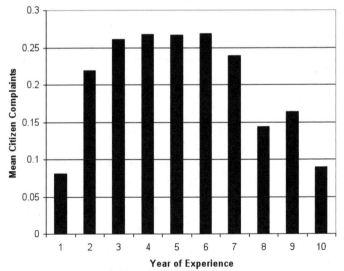

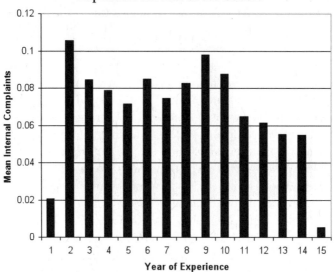

Figure 4.5 Average Internal Complaints by Year of Experience for Late 1980s Cohort

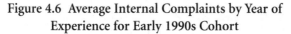

Figure 4.6 Average Internal Complaints by Year of Experience for Early 1990s Cohort

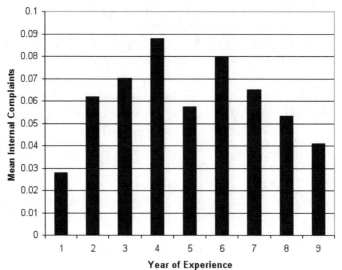

Somewhat surprisingly, the Late 1980s cohort shows an almost W-shaped curve for internal complaints over time, while the Early 1990s cohort displays an inverted W-shaped curve. These patterns, however, are displayed across very small average complaints per year, from a range of about .02 to .10 across careers. Therefore, any shape has extremely limited variation from year-to-year, and so does not warrant too much emphasis on the overall shape of the curve. Generally, both display an early peak with a general declining trend thereafter, similar to that of personnel and citizen complaints. As with the citizen complaint patterns, the internal complaint patterns for patrol officers only (not presented) differ little from their respective cohort patterns which considers all officers.

The finding of an experience-misconduct curve at the aggregate level when considering complaints filed against officers is a significant one. Such a pattern has been alluded to in the policing literature, but research has yet to establish such a pattern using longitudinal data covering within-officer change. If this finding is replicated elsewhere, it could represent a stable relationship in the policing realm, similar to that of the age-crime curve discussed previously in the criminological literature.

But one must wonder what is driving this curve, particularly the drop-off in personnel complaints after year six in both cohorts. The early rise and peak of the curve is expected given extant theory and research, and to some extent so is a steady decline, but why the general drop after year six? Part of this may have to do with other career elements, especially initiation rates. Another explanation, however, might be attributable to other behavioral phenomenon, such as productivity.

Partial support for this notion can be found in Figures 4.7 and 4.8, which displays arrest rates of patrol officers in their respective cohorts. These rates are based on only a sample of cohort members, but nevertheless the curves based on productivity and experience do tend to somewhat mirror the experience-misconduct curves. To some extent then, the experience-misconduct curve may be driven in part by productivity: as officers gain experience, they become less productive, thus making them less susceptible to com-

Figure 4.7 Average Arrests by Year of Experience for
Late 1980s Cohort

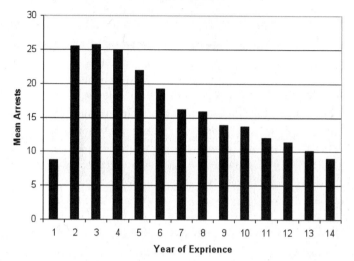

Figure 4.8 Average Arrests by Year of Experience for
Early 1990s Cohort

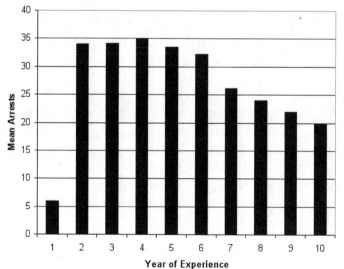

plaints. However, given that arrest rates do not drop by a significant amount over time, one might speculate that the experience-misconduct curve might be driven by factors other than productivity decline. What's more, the year-to-year correlations between citizen complaints and penal law arrests, while often statistically significant, never exceed .25, and so are weak at best.

The findings above have implications for police administrators. First, as has been suspected, officers tend to get into trouble early. Administrators would be wise to more closely monitor officers within their complaint-prone years, especially years 3–6, and deploy resources more effectively to combat problem behaviors during those years. Given that complaints are relatively rare events, and that complaint rates on average are very low, having information about when officers are most likely to encounter such problems is valuable. Second, even in the absence of a specific intervention, officers are likely to decrease their complaint rates over time. Some of this decrease might be attributed to routine supervision already established within the organization. As officers begin to accumulate above average complaint totals, supervisors may take note and formally or informally monitor and counsel officers as needed in an attempt to improve their field performance. Conversely, the threats or disciplinary action taken after officers receive multiple complaints might be enough to deter officers from repeating mistakes. Either way, already established supervision within the agency might account for the decline in average officer complaint rates over time, and thus appears to be working as intended.

The experience-misconduct curve also has implication for researchers. While many studies of police behavior includes experience as a control variable, any analysis of interventions must also take into account the general decline in problem behaviors by officers over time. Increasingly, police departments are using EIS to identify problematic officers and flag them for some sort of intervention. Some of these interventions may include a training program for officers which attempts to ameliorate problems officers may be having in the field (Kenney et al., 2001). Any evaluation of such a program, which presumably would contain officers with higher-than-average complaint rates, must take into account the experience-misconduct curve. That is, officers might exhibit a decline when comparing post-intervention rates of complaints to pre-intervention rates, but given the experience-misconduct curve, such a decline would be expected. One must be attentive to the alternative hypothesis that it is not the intervention that had an impact on declining complaint rates for problematic officers, but rather it is simply a decline over time one would expect even in the absence of a specific intervention.

Misconduct Career Elements

Having explored generally the shape of the experience-misconduct curves for different complaint types, the next series of analyses explore the various career misconduct elements such as participation, frequency, average year of onset, etc.[3,4] Recall that interest primarily lies in whether prevalence or incidence presents more of a challenge to administrators. That is, whether problem behaviors are widely prevalent in the organization as a whole, or whether it is concentrated within a small group of officers (or, possibly both).

The first career element to examine is participation, of which there are two types. The first is *cumulative participation*, which is the percentage of officers who have *ever* received a citizen complaint in their career. The results are similar for both cohorts: about

---

3. A series of analyses were conducted to test the assumption that the career elements of both cohorts are identical, except that the Late 1980s cohort had served for a longer portion of the observation period than the Early 1990s cohort. The results, based on truncating the years of experience in the Late 1980s cohort to match those of the Early 1990s cohort, support this assumption.

4. Since the results from the experience misconduct curves were virtually identical when considering all officers or only patrol officers, the rest of the analyses reported herein considers all officers. Also, these analyses consider all officers regardless of career length, since analyses excluding officers with incomplete career data were virtually indistinguishable from those presented here.

two-thirds of officers from each cohort receive at least one personnel complaint during the observation period. If a complaint is received, the likelihood is high that it will be a citizen complaint, as few officers (about one-quarter to one-third, depending on the cohort) ever received an internal complaint during the study period. Relatedly, about one-quarter to one-third of officers received *both* an internal and a citizen complaint sometime during their career. Certainly welcomed news for administrators of this agency is that about one-third of officers have never received a complaint of any kind during the study period. While cumulative participation appears to be quite high, one might suspect an even greater percentage of officers would have a complaint lodged against them had complete career data been available.

Figure 4.9 displays the cumulative participation of officers across years of experience. Thus, this figure displays the proportion of the cohort populations that ever received a complaint. As one can see,

Figure 4.9 Prevalence of Personnel Complaints by Year of Experience

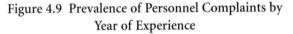

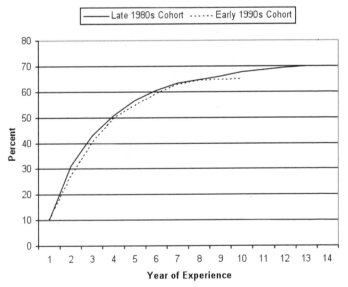

the prevalence increases sharply across the first six years of experience and begins to flatten out thereafter. For example, the Late 1980s cohort's cumulative participation for the first two years of experience is 31 percent, it then increases to 61 percent by year six, but then only increases slightly to 66 percent by year nine, and 70 percent by year fourteen. The pattern for the Early 1990s cohort is very similar.

Table 4.1 explores the *conditional initiation rates* of officers, which is the fraction that x-year of experience initiators represent of the total x-year of experience officers who have not yet received a complaint.[5] When examining the conditional initiation

Table 4.1 Conditional Initiation Rates by Complaint Type

Year of Experience	Late 1980s Cohort		Early 1990s Cohort	
	Citizen Complaints	Internal Complaints	Citizen Complaints	Internal Complaints
1	.09	.02	.08	.03
2	.19	.08	.15	.05
3	.16	.05	.14	.05
4	.11	.05	.14	.06
5	.08	.03	.09	.03
6	.06	.03	.09	.04
7	.03	.04	.06	.05
8	.04	.04	.04	.03
9	.04	.04	.02	.01
10	.02	.03	.01	.00
11	.03	.02	—	—
12	.02	.02	—	—
13	.01	.01	—	—
14	.00	.01	—	—
15	.00	.00	—	—
N =	1427	1427	718	718

5. For example, in a cohort of 1,000 officers, if 200 have received a complaint by their 1st year of experience and 100 more begin their misconduct career in their 2nd year of experience, then the initiation rate of

rates for the two cohorts in the table, one can observe that past year six, very few officers receive their first personnel complaint. In fact, the initiation rates match that of the aggregate curve, with these rates peaking early in officers' careers, and with a steadily decreasing number of initiators with each successive year following the peak. So, while having complete career data is desirable, each additional year is unlikely to add to a significant increase in prevalence, since most officers are detected for problem behaviors early in their careers.

This idea is also supported when examining onset, which is presented in Table 4.2 for all three complaint types for the respective cohorts. For both cohorts, onset for personnel and citizen complaints is the middle-to-late part of the third year of experience. This means that most officers obtain their first complaint around the point at which the experience-misconduct curve peaks, which is expected if participation is driving the curve. The onset of internal complaints for both cohorts is somewhat later than citizen complaints. This might reflect the notion that officers are very unlikely to report the misconduct of fellow officers, so that the average chance of an internal complaint is much lower than that of a citizen complaint, given an ob-

Table 4.2 Average Year of Onset

	Late 1980s Cohort		Early 1990s Cohort	
	All Officers	Active Only	All Officers	Active Only
Onset				
Personnel Complaints	3.7 (n = 1000)	2.9 (n = 610)	3.3 (n = 466)	2.6 (n = 207)
Citizen Complaints	3.9 (n = 923)	3.0 (n = 480)	3.5 (n = 414)	2.6 (n = 150)
Internal Complaints	5.7 (n = 551)	4.1 (n = 133)	4.3 (n = 216)	3.1 (n = 22)

the officers in their 2nd year is $100/1000 = .10$ and their conditional initiation rate is $100/(1,000-200) = .1244$.

served act of misconduct. If this is accurate, then one would expect the average onset of internal complaints to be later, since the chance of such a complaint is lower in the aggregate.

Overall, it appears that prevalence is fairly high, with a majority of officers obtaining at least one personnel complaint over the course of their career. Thus, the quick rise and steady decline in the experience-misconduct curve could be comprised of a large number of initiators in the early years of experience, with fewer and fewer officers initiating in the later years of experience. If the modal officer career is 20 years (the career service length at which officers can retire with full pension), then most officers will initiate misconduct during the first quarter of their career. This relationship is largely driven by citizen complaints, as relatively few officers will receive an internal complaint in their career.

Despite the prevalence of misconduct as measured by personnel complaints, there were a non-trivial number of officers for whom no complaints were ever filed. Nearly one-third of the officers in the Late 1980s cohort did not receive a complaint during the observation period. This number would unlikely change had complete career data been available, or if it did change, such a number would be unlikely to change dramatically, given the observed onset and initiation rates. Whether these officers are highly skilled in their assignments, or simply skilled at avoiding complaints, remains an empirical question for future research.

There is also the question of how often officers engage in misconduct once they initiate, and for how long. To estimate frequency, the example of Blumstein et al. (1986) is followed and the incidence of misconduct is estimated by removing the first complaint as a measure of onset (thus demonstrating an officer is "active"), and the last complaint (marking a "desistance" point) to estimate the number of years an officer was active. A complaint frequency rate is then calculated for officers by examining their remaining complaints across years active during the study period. This calculation requires that officers have at least three complaints across their career, which is somewhat problematic, given that officers with two or fewer complaints are not considered. If an officer has received only one complaint, they are active in misconduct, but because of incomplete career data, the officer has no demonstration of a desistance point.[6] If an officer receives two complaints, his/her last year served is used as a desistance point, but only if the officer left the agency before the study period ended.[7] The notion of false desistance looms, however, due to incomplete career data, as it does with all longitudinal studies of deviance that do not consider the entire careers of subjects.

When examining personnel complaints, about one-third of the officers have no complaints during their career, and 15 percent and 22 percent have only one complaint filed against them in the Late 1980s cohort and the Early 1990s cohort, respectively. This means that 44.5 percent of the officers in the Late 1980s cohort and 57 percent of the officers in the Early 1990s cohort, the concept of frequency is not applicable and thus an inappropriate statistic. Again, this demonstrates if officers do receive a complaint, the complaint total will be low, and most likely will be only one complaint. In fact, while some officers do receive as many as 10 complaints in their career (and in two cases in the Early 1980s cohort, as many as 21), the vast majority of officers who do have complaints (75 percent) obtain less than four. The requirement of at least three personnel complaints to calculate frequency significantly limits the number of officers available for analysis: only 610 officers from the Late 1980s cohort and 207 officers from the Early 1990s cohort are analyzed with regards to their personnel complaints. Considering only citizen or internal complaints reduces the number of officers even further.

Table 4.2 also displays the average year of onset for the limited number of officers for whom frequency is estimated. Interestingly,

---

6. Blumstein and his colleagues never provide an adequate response to the criticism that the criminal career paradigm cannot be adequately applied to someone who commits only 1 criminal act in their lifetime, other than to argue such an offender does not exist.

7. This allowed retention of only a handful of addition cases (5–18, depending on the cohort and complaint type). The results when using these cases compared to results using only officers with three or more complaints are virtually identical.

for each cohort and for each complaint type, onset is earlier for these officers. That is, officers with three or more complaints (or two or more complaints for those who left early) have an average earlier onset date when compared to officers with only one or two complaints. This suggests that officers who receive greater numbers of citizen and internal complaints, that is, officers who are more problematic, start their career in problem behaviors earlier than officers who are less problematic or not problematic at all.

Table 4.3 further explores the relationship between year of onset and the average number of personnel complaint received by officers in their respective cohorts. As can been seen, officers demonstrating an earlier age of onset are more likely to receive a greater average number of personnel complaints than officers exhibiting a later onset date. Part of this variation between year of onset and accumulation of complaints is due to length of observation, as those

Table 4.3 Personnel Complaints by Year of Onset

	Late 1980s Cohort			Early 1990s Cohort	
Year of Onset	Mean Number of Complaints	Number of Officers	Year of Onset	Mean Number of Complaints	Number of Officers
1	5.2	149	1	3.8	74
2	5.2	295	2	3.5	122
3	4.5	170	3	3.1	92
4	3.5	108	4	2.5	68
5	2.9	85	5	2.2	36
6	2.9	56	6	1.4	33
7	2.3	40	7	1.5	25
8	2.4	22	8	1.3	12
9	1.7	20	9	1.0	3
10	1.4	20	10	1.0	1
11	1.5	15			
12	1.5	12			
13	1.3	7			
14	1.0	1			

who begin misconduct earlier have more time to accumulate complaints. Still, the table demonstrates a clear tendency of early starters to engage in more problematic behaviors. This is interesting in that it parallels the criminal career research which demonstrates that individuals with an early age of onset tend to commit crimes at higher rates than those with a later age of onset (Loeber and Snyder, 1990).

Table 4.4 shows the average frequency rate for the various complaint types for active officers by cohort. When frequency is calculated for the active officers in each cohort by complaint type, one finds that the rates at which officers receive complaints is quite low, averaging less than one complaint per year for each type. For each cohort, citizen complaint rates are greater than internal complaint rates.

Table 4.4 also displays a column for adjusted citizen complaint rates. In an attempt to correct for bias in official data for those officers who received a citizen complaint during the observation period, a misconduct rate (μ), or the actual number of misconduct acts committed by an officer, is calculated based on the officer's complaint rate (λ) and their risk for complaints (q). Chapter 2 noted that Walker and Bumphus (1992) estimate approximately two-thirds of all police misconduct goes unreported by citizens. This, in essence, could be utilized as an estimation of the probability of a citizen complaint once misconduct has occurred (q), essentially giving a "citizen complaint risk" of .3. This correction is utilized in the frequency estimations of misconduct (μ), and so comparisons can be made with corrected ver-

Table 4.4 Average Annual Frequency Rates for Active Officers

Frequency	Late 1980s Cohort	Early 1990s Cohort
Personnel Complaints	.59	.73
	(n = 610)	(n = 207)
Citizen Complaints	.51	.67
	(n = 480)	(n = 150)
Adjusted Citizen	1.7	2.2
Complaints	(n = 480)	(n = 150)
Internal Complaints	.48	.75
	(n = 133)	(n = 22)

sus uncorrected data to examine how it changes individual frequency rates of misconduct.

Internal complaints yield different frequencies. Given that no officer in either cohort obtained more than nine internal complaints during their career, this is not surprising. In fact, 99 percent of officers received five or fewer internal complaints, and the vast majority (over 80 percent in both cohorts) received only one. Notice the estimations for the Early 1990s cohort are based on only 22 cases, which accounts for the exceedingly high rates for this particular type of complaint, as nearly half of those officers had a rate of one or more internal complaints while active.

Given these estimations, one can estimate the frequency for the average officer who is actively engaged in misconduct across the study period. The average duration of misconduct activity measured by complaints are presented in Table 4.5 for both cohorts. For personnel complaints, the average career length for misconduct was 7.1 years in the Late 1980s cohort and 4.1 years in the Early 1990s cohort. So, for the Late 1980s cohort, given an average career length of 7.1 years and an average personnel complaint rate of .59 per year, the average active officer would receive 4.2 complaints while active. For the Early 1990s cohort, the average active officer would receive 3 complaints while active.

Examining the same frequency pattern for citizen complaints, the average career length for the Late 1980s cohort was 6.6 years, meaning the average active officers would receive 3.4 citizen complaints while active. The average career length for the Early 1990s

Table 4.5 Average Duration of Careers for Active Officers

Duration	Late 1980s Cohort	Early 1990s Cohort
Personnel Complaints	7.0	4.1
	(n = 610)	(n = 207)
Citizen Complaints	6.6	4.2
	(n = 480)	(n = 150)
Internal Complaints	5.3	3.2
	(n = 133)	(n = 22)

cohort for citizen complaints was 4.2 years, giving the average active officers in this cohort 2.8 complaints while active. Finally, the frequency for internal complaints for active officers can also be estimated. The average career length for internal complaints was 5.3 years for the Late 1980s cohort and 3.2 years for the Early 1990s cohort. This provides frequency rate estimations of 2.5 and 2.4 for the average active officers in their respective cohorts while active during the study period.

Keep in mind that these estimates are based on incomplete career data, making estimations of career length and frequency biased, presuming that officers with additional career data would have longer durations and additional complaints to consider. The strength of these estimations, however, is that they do consider the years when officers are most at-risk for complaints. While each additional year of data is not bound to radically alter the aggregate estimations, given that most officers start their careers early, it is not possible to accurately estimate desistance, duration, and frequency with incomplete career data.[8] Interpretations of these data must therefore proceed with caution.

Given these frequency estimations, and the estimations of participation, one can see that while many officers engage in problem behaviors, those who do participate do so at relatively low rates. In fact, most officers receive only one or two personnel complaints during the study period, if they receive any. However, the few officers who do receive multiple personnel complaints still do not typically exceed more than one complaint per year on average. In fact, only about 10 to 15 percent of officers in both cohorts had an average frequency rate of one or more personnel complaints a year when active. Very few, less than 3 percent in both cohorts, had an average annual frequency rate of two or more personnel complaints per year. Still, consistent with previous research, as small percentage of officers account for a disproportionate amount of personnel

---

8. One might suspect that rates of personnel complaints will increase near or after the point at which officers can retire with a full pension.

complaints: the top 10 percent or so of officers with complaints account for about one-third of all complaints.

One must remember, however, that these estimations also undercount the actual amount of misconduct recorded. The true frequency rates of officers actively engaged in misconduct are most likely higher than the estimations presented here. One can begin to glimpse this idea by using the adjusted average frequency estimations for citizen complaints for the cohorts. Recall from Tables 4.4 and 4.5 that active officers in the late 1980s cohort had an average adjusted annual frequency of 1.7, and an average career length of 6.6 years. This means that the average active officer had an adjusted frequency rate of 11.2 citizen complaints for the duration of their observed career for this cohort. Also, recall that active officers in the Early 1990s cohort had an average adjusted annual frequency rate of 2.2 and an average career length of 4.2 years. This means that the average active officer had an adjusted frequency rate of 9.2 citizen complaints for the duration of their observed career for this cohort. These estimations are quite high, much more so when compared to the unadjusted estimations of 3.4 complaints while active on average for the Late 1980s cohort and 2.8 complaints while active on average for the Early 1990s cohort.

Conclusion

What is to be concluded from this initial series of analyses? First, experience and misconduct appear to be related in an orderly way. Misconduct peaks quickly and early in officers' careers, and begins a steady decline thereafter. The average onset of misconduct for both cohorts was in the later half of year three for both personnel and citizen complaints, with internal complaints having a much later onset date. In addition, the shape of the curve appears to be driven largely by prevalence, since most officers receive at least one personnel complaint in their career. That is, the peak and steady decline is likely due to a large number of initiators in the early years of experience, and a steady declining number of initiators afterwards, with fewer and fewer officers beginning their misconduct careers beyond the fifth or sixth year of experience.

Second, persistent misconduct is infrequent. While most officers will receive a personnel complaint sometime in their career, few will obtain multiple complaints. In both cohorts, about a one-quarter to one-third of officers who receive a personnel complaint obtain only one. Over one-half the officers with a personnel complaint have three or fewer, and over three-quarters of the officers have five or fewer personnel complaints. Very few officers obtain a large number of complaints, or average one complaint or more per year when active. One implication of this finding is that problem officers, if one defines them as officers who are chronically problematic over their career course (i.e., have a long duration and high frequency), will be very small in number when compared to the overall population of officers. This is likely welcomed news for the agency, given that problem behaviors are fairly prevalent in the organization, but do not occur with a high degree of frequency. This does pose a challenge, however, in that administrators do not have a specific group upon which to target interventions since officers who are problematic at one point in time are unlikely to be problematic again.

Nevertheless, the question remains: might there be specific trajectories which underlie the aggregate experience-misconduct curve? There are certainly a number of officers who receive multiple complaints available for analyses, so might these officers follow differing pathways? Specifically, would we find a problem officer group who offend at consistently high rates over their career course? The series of trajectory analyses described in the following two chapters attempts to address these important questions.

Chapter 5

Trajectories of Citizen Complaints

The next question central to this investigation is whether there exist specific career pathways that underlie the aggregate relationship between experience and misconduct. Research on police deviance provides two differing views: either there is a uniform pathway in misconduct, with all officers behaving in more-or-less the same way, or multiple pathways in misconduct, with officers differing in their patterns of problem behaviors over time. Relating to the latter hypothesis, three distinct trajectories are proposed, based upon relatively sparse police research: (1) an abstainer group, or officers who are not involved in misconduct; (2) a problem officer group, or officers who are involved in numerous allegations of misconduct by citizens throughout their career; and (3) a group of officers who follow the aggregate experience-misconduct curve.

Analyses begin with citizen complaints for the Late 1980s cohort using Nagin's (2005) semiparametric, group-based approach. This approach has been useful in criminology in validating typologies of antisocial behavior over time, and thus will prove beneficial here in assessing whether there are multiple career paths in misconduct underlying the aggregate experience-misconduct curves. Specifically, this chapter examines the citizen complaint trajectories of the 1138 officers from the Late 1980s cohort, who served between 1 and 14.5 years, and the 613 officers from the Early 1990s cohort, who served between 1 and 10.5 years. The analyses also assess how emerging trajectory groups (1) differ on specific misconduct career dimensions, (2) whether demographic or background characteristics distinguish between the trajectory groups, and (3) whether the trajectories differ in terms of their correlates of civil litigation, uses of force, and arrest rates.

Trajectory Analyses Using the Semiparametric, Group-Based Approach

The general procedure for utilizing the semiparametric, group-based approach involves three steps.[1] First is to estimate the optimal number of trajectory groups that underlie the cohorts based on citizen complaints of officers over their careers. Because count data are employed here, the Poisson model is appropriate. However, in the Late 1980s cohort more zeros are present than would be expected based on the Poisson distribution, so the zero-inflated Poisson (ZIP) distribution is used. The Early 1990s cohort employs the purely Poisson model.

To evaluate model fit, previous research is followed and uses the Bayesian Information Criterion (BIC). The BIC tends to favor more parsimonious models when compared to likelihood ratio tests for model selection. The BIC is calculated as:

$$BIC = \log(L) - 0.5k\log(N)$$

Where L is the model's maximized likelihood vale, N is the sample size, and k is the number of model parameters, specifically the order of the polynomial and the number of groups used (Nagin, 2005). An iterative procedure is used whereby increasingly larger numbers of groups are added to the model to maximize the BIC. The

---

1. A special procedure for use in SAS called Proc Traj, developed by Jones et al. (2001), is employed for trajectory estimation. The Proc Traj procedure, and related documentation, is available online: http://www.andrew. cmu.edu/user/bjones.

trajectories are also estimated using four different polynomials (intercept-only, linear, quadratic, and cubic) in order to determine which best characterizes the trajectories of officers in both cohorts.[2] Once the number of groups is decided upon, the second step involves sorting the cohort members into their respective trajectories using the highest posterior probability of group membership. Based on these probabilities, officers are assigned to the trajectory that best fits their misconduct histories. This allows exploration of the "average" characteristics of each trajectory, creating profiles of group membership. Profiles using the demographic and background characteristics of the officers in both cohorts are constructed.

This step also provides a second calculation, the average posterior probability (AvePP) of assignment, which is useful in assessing the quality of the model's fit to the data (Nagin, 2005). Once officers are assigned to the trajectory that best matches their actual complaint history, one ideally wants the probability that each officer is assigned to their best-fitting group to be 1. This is seldom the case, although models with similar fits to the data (e.g., similar BICs) can be assessed in terms of which ones provide better AvePPs of assignment. While Nagin's (2005, p. 88) "rule of thumb" is that all groups in a model have an AvePP of assignment greater than .7 to be adequate, models whose groups have AvePPs of assignment closer to 1 do a better job of placing individuals in trajectory groups than competing models, and thus would be more desirable.

For the third step, the percentage of the population in each latent trajectory group is estimated. This can be thought of as the probability that a randomly chosen individual will follow a particular trajectory. The trajectory results from both cohorts are presented below.

----

2. It is the case here that varying polynomials provide similarly reasonable fits to the data. While the decision of the final model is based on formal criteria such as the BIC and AvePP, it was also based on police theories and domain knowledge of police misconduct.

Trajectories of Citizen Complaints for the Late 1980s Cohort

In selecting the number of groups underlying the curve, testing was done for one, two, three, four, five, and six groups employing a cubic polynomial.[3] The cubic function linking experience and misconduct is ideal for this cohort because it can take into account the quick rise and gradual decline that was seen in the aggregate experience-misconduct curve. Table 5.1 displays the BIC values for the different number of trajectory groups. As can be seen, the model improves substantially when a second group is added, improves slightly with the addition of a third group, and declines with addition of a fourth group. The five and six group models (not shown) also lower the BIC, noting a decline in model fit. When examining the plots, the two-group model differentiated between a low- and a high-rate group. The three-group model differentiated between a mid-rate group approximating the experience-misconduct curve, a higher-rate group, and a low-rate group. The four-group model does not reveal any important additional features to the data, and

Table 5.1 BIC Values for Cubic Estimates for the Late 1980s Cohort

Number of Groups	Cubic
1	-8121.83
2	-7784.19
3	-7778.72*
4	-7782.77
* Best fit by BIC criterion	

---

3. Since the officer-complaint file can distinguish between years where officers received zero complaints and years where officers had left the agency before the observation period ended, analyses consider years after the officer had left as missing data.

three of the groups' AvePPs of assignment fell below .7. Therefore, analyses are based on a three-group model.[4]

Table 5.2a presents the parameter estimates for the selected model, and Table 5.2b presents the posterior probabilities for group assignment. The AvePPs for the three-group model are adequate, but the model struggles somewhat between placing officers into the low- and the mid-rate groups. Thus, this model does not perform as well many models in criminology which typically have AvePPs of group assignment of .8 or greater for all groups.

Figure 5.1a displays the predicted trajectories identified and estimated for the Late 1980s cohort. The Figures 5.1b–5.1d display the shape of the actual and predicted trajectory for each of the three groups. The discussion of these trajectories will focus on the predicted paths, as these are easier to view due to their smooth course.

Only one of the three trajectories expected to underlie the experience-misconduct curve was found; the other two displayed different patterns than was anticipated. The first group, and the one expected to emerge, approximates the aggregate experience-misconduct curve. These officers, who are labeled the mid-rate trajectory, comprise about 36 percent of the cohort.[5] The results also find a trajectory that one might liken to problem officers, but such officers do not peak and continue to offend at high rates over their career course. Instead, this group—who are labeled the high-rate trajectory—peaks and declines at almost the same rate, but they do peak later than their peers in the other two trajectories, and have greater numbers of citizen complaints per year.[6] As expected, this group comprises a small percentage of the cohort, only 5 per-

---

4. Consideration of only patrol officers or all officers regardless of rank produced nearly identical results, so the analyses consider all officers regardless of rank.

5. The trajectory labels are not meant to reify the existence of these groups, but as a means of discussion rather than using more abstract labels (e.g., group 1, group 2, group 3).

6. A series of analyses focusing on a subset of citizen complaint categories designed to better isolate problem officer behaviors (e.g., excessive

cent. Surprisingly, there was no "abstainer" group found. Instead, a group engaging in a very low-level of misconduct was found who comprised about 59 percent of the population.[7] This last group of officers is labeled the low-rate trajectory.[8]

Table 5.3 presents the various misconduct career dimensions of the three trajectory groups.[9] As can be seen from this table, the three groups differ from each other in important, but expected, ways. There were a total of 3,070 citizen complaints filed against the officers in the Late 1980s cohort during the study period. The vast majority of these complaints were filed against officers from the mid-rate group, who accounted for nearly 60 percent of all complaints filed. The remaining complaints are evenly accounted for by the low- and high-rate groups, who each account for about one-fifth of the citizen complaints. Keep in mind, however, that the officers are not evenly distributed across trajectory groups. The high-rate officers, who comprise only 5 percent of the cohort, account for almost as large a percentage of citizen complaints as the low-rate officers, who account for nearly 60 percent of the cohort population. The mid-rate officers also account for a large share of the misconduct, comprising a little more than one-third of the cohort, but accounting for more than one-half of all the citizen complaints filed.

---

force, discourtesy, etc.) were attempted to better distill a problem officer trajectory. Since this limited the already small number of citizen complaints, the three-group trajectory model fit declined, and while a high-rate trajectory was still found, it did not exhibit a significantly different path than is presented above.

7. This group does, however, contain all of the officers with no citizen complaints filed against them.

8. One might expect that officers entering in different years may disproportionately comprise one of the trajectory groups, since officers entering earlier have more time to generate complaints. This was not found—there are no significant differences in the composition of the trajectory groups based on year of entry.

9. The results presented in this table were inspired by Piquero et al. (2005) who conducted similar analyses with the six trajectories emerging from the Cambridge Study in Delinquent Development data.

Table 5.2a Parameter Estimates and Group Assignment Probabilities for the Late 1980s Cohort

Group	Parameter	Estimate	SE	T
1	Intercept	-1.393	0.356	-3.914
	Linear	-0.009	0.231	-0.043
	Quadratic	-0.411	0.039	-1.061
	Cubic	0.003	0.002	1.420
2	Intercept	-0.907	0.247	-3.678
	Linear	0.11	0.133	1.504
	Quadratic	-0.051	0.021	-2.428
	Cubic	0.003	0.001	2.484
3	Intercept	-0.648	0.4	-1.621
	Linear	0.283	0.203	1.391
	Quadratic	-0.033	0.032	-1.028
	Cubic	0.001	0.002	0.537
	Alpha0	1.582	0.556	2.843
	Alpha1	-1.401	0.384	-3.644
	Alpha2	0.094	0.022	4.244
	BIC = -7778.717 (n = 1138)			
Group Membership				
1	(%)	51.491	7.356	7.0
2	(%)	41.871	6.184	6.771
3	(%)	6.638	2.18	3.052

Table 5.2b Posterior Probabilities for Group Assignments for the Late 1980s Cohort

Groups	Low-Rate	Mid-Rate	High-Rate
Low-Rate	.80	.17	.00
Mid-Rate	.20	.76	.17
High-Rate	.00	.07	.83

Figure 5.1a Three Group Predicted Trajectory Model for Late 1980s Cohort

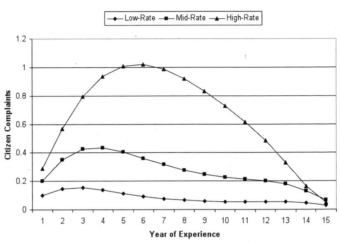

Figure 5.1b Low-Rate Trajectory for the Late 1980s Cohort

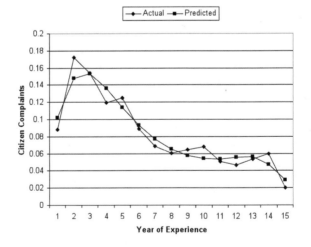

Figure 5.1c Mid-Rate Trajectory for Late 1980s Cohort

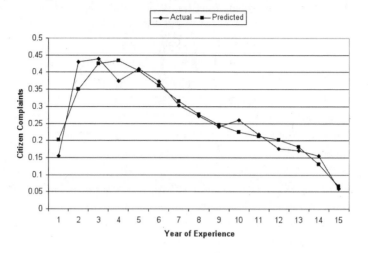

Figure 5.1d High-Rate Trajectory for Late 1980s Cohort

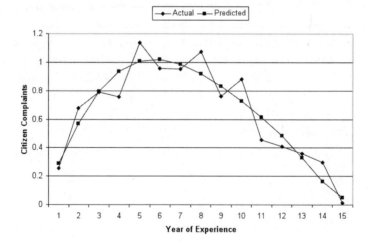

Table 5.3 Citizen Complaint Trajectories and Misconduct
Elements for Late 1980s Cohort

Variable	Low-Rate (n = 670)	Mid-Rate (n = 407)	High-Rate (n = 61)
Cohort Member (%)	58.9	35.8	5.4
Total number of complaints	699	1761	610
Mean number of complaints	1.0	4.3	10
Cohort complaints (%)	22.8	57.4	19.9
Mean year of onset	4.6	3.3	2.5
Number of problem officers (6+ citizen complaints)	0	37	57
Number of active officers	34	385	61
Mean frequency	.28	.45	1.1
Mean career length	6.6	6.5	8.1
Mean year of desistance	8.8	9.5	10.6

As expected, the officers in the high-rate groups average more complaints across their careers than either the mid- or low-rate group. Not only do high-rate officers average more acts of misconduct, their mean year of experience for onset is earlier than the other groups, and is two years earlier than the low-rate group. If we employ the Christopher Commission's (1991) definition of a problem officer as one who receives six or more citizen complaints in five years, it is not surprising that most officers in the high-rate group would be a problem officer, while none of the officers in the low-rate group could be labeled as such.[10] The mid-rate trajectory also contains some problem officers, suggesting the label of a problem officer is too broad to capture important differences in officer misconduct.

10. It should be noted that the Christopher Commission only examined citizen complaints of excessive force and not all citizen complaints as is done here.

Examining the dimensions of "active" officers also illustrates the differences in misconduct between the trajectory groups. Not only did the high-rate group have an earlier onset, but their desistance point is later, and hence their career duration longer, than either the mid- or low-rate groups. Also, the high-rate trajectory's average frequency of citizen complaints is greater than either of the other two trajectory groups. The mid- and low-rate trajectory groups were somewhat similar in their career dimensions of duration and desistance, even though the mid-rate group has, as one might expect, a greater frequency.

In short, misconduct is not static, nor is it uniform across officer careers, as is seen here. While experience and misconduct are related in an orderly way in the aggregate, officers differ in their patterns of problematic behavior over time in important ways. While no evidence of a problem officer group (who peaks early and has a steadily high frequency and no desistance point) was found, a high-rate group who begins earlier, peaks and desists later, and engages in a greater frequency of misconduct than the other groups was uncovered. Whether administrators would consider this group as "problem officers" remains to be seen, but the high-rate and the mid-rate groups are certainly problematic enough to warrant further empirical investigation.

Profiles of Citizen Complaints for the Late 1980s Cohort

Now that the optimal number of trajectories has been decided upon, and cohort members have been assigned to the trajectory they are most likely to belong to based on their behavior, the profiles of the various groups can be examined. Particular interest lies in whether the low-rate trajectory differs in terms of its demographic profile when compared to the other two higher-rate trajectories.

Table 5.4 displays the demographic and background characteristics for the low-, mid-, and high-rate officer trajectories.[11] As
might be anticipated based on problem officer research, the high-
rate group tends to be predominately male. Also in line with some
previous research, the more problematic officers in this cohort tend
not to be White. In fact, Whites make up only 60 percent of the
high-rate trajectory, which is quite low given that Whites are the
predominant racial group in the cohort. Blacks on the other hand

Table 5.4 Profiles of Citizen Complaint Trajectories for the Late 1980s Cohort

Demographic Variables	Low-Rate (n = 670)	Mid-Rate (n = 407)	High-Rate (n = 61)
Cohort			
% of Population	58.9	35.8	5.4
Gender			
Male (%)	87.9	93.1	98.4
Female (%)	15.2	6.9	1.6
Total	100.0	100.0	100.0
Race			
White (%)	79.0	65.8	59.0
Black (%)	11.8	20.4	32.8
Hispanic (%)	8.5	13.5	8.2
Other (%)	0.7	0.3	0.0
Total	100.0	100.0	100.0
Background Characteristics			
Military Service (%)	5.6	7.4	14.8
No Military Service (%)	91.9	92.6	85.2
Total	100.0	100.0	100.0
College Degree (%)	53.6	43.0	26.2
No College Degree (%)	46.4	57.0	73.8
Total	100.0	100.0	100.0

11. Mean age at entry is not included in these analyses as it did not
vary by trajectory group.

are much more likely to be in the high-rate group. This is not true of all minority officers, as Hispanics and officers in the Other category are less likely to be in the mid- or high-rate groups.

Why might Black officers increasingly comprise the higher-rate misconduct trajectories? The most obvious hypothesis is that Blacks perform worse in police-citizen encounters than other racial groups.[12] To the extent that Black officers are found to be more proactive, this could also account for the difference in performance. Or, since this particular agency was ordered to hire more minority officers during the early 1980s, perhaps they admitted some officers based more on minority status than on performance potential, which may also account for these results.[13] An alternative hypothesis such as that posed by Lersch and Mieczkowski (1996) would be that citizens are more likely to complain against Black officers. Since this police department serves a predominately White citizenry, this might very well be the case.[14] Given that officers are often involved in confrontational encounters with citizens, if White citizens were more likely to file complaints against Black officers—all else being equal—one would expect this finding. The data provide no means to test the second or third hypothesis, and the two are not necessarily mutually exclusive. The hypothesis that Black officers are more proactive was not supported, as their arrest rates in the sample of officers with penal law arrest data were the lowest when compared to white and Hispanic officers.

Support is found for the hypothesis that higher-rate officers are more likely to have served in the military prior to their becoming a police officer. The hypothesis that while military personnel would

---

12. This is not to suggest that race has a direct effect on performance, as race is instead better understood as a proxy for numerous social indicators (socioeconomic status, etc.).

13. For example, Black officers were found to contain the lowest percentage of officers without a college degree when compared to the other racial groups.

14. The personnel complaint data unfortunately do not contain demographic information on the complainant, so this hypothesis cannot be tested.

likely adapt readily to the paramilitary structure of the police, they may have trouble with serving a civilian population is supported when examining citizen complaints: the high-rate trajectory group has the largest percentage of officers with prior military experience. A difference in education amongst the trajectory groups is also found. Officers with college degrees tend to be found in the mid- and low-level complaint trajectories when compared to the high-rate group. Of course, this variable only indicates that an officer received a degree prior to, or sometime during, the course of their career. Thus, there exists a problem of temporal ordering, as education while on the job is a correlate, yet education prior to employment can be considered a protective factor. However, if one instead views education as a constellation of traits, such as interest in career advancement, ambition, or even an internal desire to excel, then temporal ordering is not an issue; it's a protective factor, thought to shield one from risk of misconduct. If one thinks of officers who obtain a college degree as those most interested in advancing their career, then finding such officers to be more likely located in the low- and mid-rate groups is not surprising.

One might be curious as to whether the differences between the trajectory groups are statistically significant. Nagin (2005) provides a method for estimating significance tests using the semiparametric, group-based approach, the results of which are displayed in Table 5.5.[15] Each coefficient estimate in the table measures how the demographic characteristics influence the probability of group membership in a particular trajectory relative to the membership in a specified comparison group. Here the comparison group is the low-rate trajectory. The table can be thought of as reporting two separate binary logistic regression analyses that contrast the mid-rate and high-rate groups with the low-rate group. A positive coefficient estimate for a specific trajectory group implies that the associated variable increases the probability of membership in that group relative to the low-rate comparison group (Nagin, 2005).

---

15. Since officers in the Other racial category contain so few officers, they are removed from analysis.

Table 5.5 Demographic Predictors of Citizen Complaint
Trajectory Membership for the Late 1980s Cohort

Variable	Coefficient Estimate	Standard Error	t-Statistic
Mid-Rate			
Male	1.04	0.40	2.76**
Black	1.02	0.30	3.42**
Hispanic	1.09	0.34	3.18**
Military	-0.68	0.44	-1.55
Degree	-0.52	0.21	-2.51**
High-Rate			
Male	1.8	1.03	1.70*
Black	1.49	0.37	3.94**
Hispanic	-0.42	1.00	-0.31
Military	0.61	0.45	1.26
Degree	-1.36	0.41	-3.22**

n = 1132
* $t < .10$
** $t < .05$

Comparison group is the low-rate trajectory

Likewise, a negative coefficient implies a decrease in relative probability. The difference between these results and results from a binary logistic regression is that Nagin's model takes into account the
probabilistic nature of the group assignments, whereas a logistic
regression assumes group assignments are deterministic.

As one can observe in the table, all of the demographic characteristics except military service serve to distinguish the mid-rate
group from the low-rate group, using an alpha of .10.[16] Thus, being
male or a minority (either Black or Hispanic) increases the prob-

16. Since this research is exploratory, the conventional alpha-level of
.05 is relaxed and .10 is used instead. However, the tables will distinguish
the two for the reader.

ability of being in the mid-rate group relative to the low-rate group. Also, earning a college degree decreases the probability of being in the mid-rate group relative to the low-rate group. All of these results are in the expected direction, except for prior military service, which is not statistically significant.

Most of the demographic characteristics also significantly distinguish the high-rate group from the low-rate group. Being male and Black increases the likelihood of membership in the high-rate group relative to the low-rate group, while obtaining a college degree decreases the probability. Surprisingly, military service appears to not affect the probability of high-rate group membership relative to the low-rate group, even though the coefficient is in the expected direction.

From these analyses one finds that all of the demographic characteristics increase the likelihood of membership in one of the higher-rate groups compared to the low-rate group, as does the background characteristic of education. Thus, females, Whites, and those with a college degree are significantly more likely to be assigned to the low-rate group. Implications from these findings are discussed below.

Correlates of Citizen Complaint Trajectories for the Late 1980s Cohort

In addition to demographic characteristics, other correlates of interest amongst the trajectory groups can be examined: this study contains data on each officer's involvement in civil litigation, each use of force incident, and, for a subset of officers, there are data on the number of penal law arrests made per year. Results from empirical analyses concerning these variables are presented below.[17]

---

17. These analyses, because they do not take into account the probabilistic nature of SPM group assignment, are subject to some unknown degree of bias. Previous work, however, has shown that inferences are

Table 5.6 Civil Litigation Involvement by Citizen Complaint Trajectory for the Late 1980s Cohort

	Trajectory Group		
Civil Litigation	Low-Rate (n = 670)	Mid-Rate (n = 407)	High-Rate (n = 61)
No Involvement (%)	83.1	67.1	55.7
Involvement (%)	16.9	32.9	44.3
Total	100.0	100.0	100.0
Chi-Square = 50.08*			
* p < .001			

Table 5.6 presents the percentages of officers involved in civil litigation for the three trajectory groups. Only about one-fifth of all officers in this cohort were ever involved in civil litigation sometime during the period for which this data was available, but this variable is not evenly distributed across trajectory groups. As expected, officers who are involved in the higher-rate trajectory groups are increasingly involved in civil litigation. In fact, in the high-rate trajectory group, nearly one-third of officers were involved in some form of civil litigation, as compared with about 17 percent of officers in the low-rate trajectory group.

Uses of force by the officers in each trajectory group were also examined. While the role of the police officer often necessitates the use of force, it is suspected that some officers tend to apply coercion to a wider range of circumstances than is required. Thus, while most officers will use force multiple times in their career—even though the frequency of such is fairly low—one might suspect that those who do so more often would indicate a proclivity towards misconduct, net of other factors.

---

scarcely affected by formal correction for group assignment uncertainty (Roeder et al., 1999).

Table 5.7 Mean Uses of Force by Trajectory for the Late 1980s Cohort

| | Trajectory Group | | | |
	Low-Rate (n = 191)	Mid-Rate (n = 179)	High-Rate (n = 30)	F-Ratio
Mean Uses of Force	2.0	2.4	4.0	22.813*

* p < .001

Table 5.7 presents the average number of uses of force during the study period for each trajectory group. Only 28.5 percent of officers in the Late 1980s cohort reported using force, which may seem low except that this data is only available for six years. The prevalence of this indicator was not equal across the trajectory groups. Less than one-third of officers in the low-rate group used force, whereas slightly less than half of the mid- and high-rate groups used force. Of those officers who used force, the mean number of uses also significantly differed by trajectory group. As expected, officers who belong to the high-rate group employed coercion more times on average than the low-rate group—nearly two times as much.[18]

Thus, officers in the higher-rate trajectories display both greater prevalence of civil litigation and use of force frequency. To the extent that variation in these indicators is partially attributable to misconduct, the findings add strength to the notion that the trajectories are sorting officers into groups based on some underlying proclivity to engage in misconduct.

---

18. Post Hoc contrasts were conducted using the Dunnett's T3 procedure. Because the data violated the assumption of homogeneity of variance, traditional follow-up tests such as the Tukey procedure could not be used. The Dunnett's T3 procedure has been found to be the most appropriate post hoc procedure when dealing with unequal variances and sample sizes when one or more of the groups have fewer than 50 cases (Dunnett, 1980). The procedure reveals that all of the trajectories significantly differ from each other in terms of their mean uses of force.

Of course, the results thus far are subject to the alternate hypothesis that citizen complaints, uses of force, and even to some extent involvement in civil litigation are all attributable to, or perhaps byproducts of, productivity. That is, officers who are proactive are going to make more arrests, and therefore receive more citizen complaints (and perhaps even civil lawsuits), and also have occasion to use force more often, than less productive officers, regardless of their actual misconduct levels. Thus, these indicators are not valid measures of misconduct, but instead are better understood as measures of productivity. The next series of analyses are designed to examine the "good apples" hypothesis of misconduct.

Recall from Chapter 3 that the EIS project was unable to collect penal law arrest data for all officers during the sample time period. Instead, this data was collected for only specific cohorts of officers — those entering in 1987, 1992, 1994 and 1996. Thus, for the Late 1980s cohort, only those officers entering in 1987 have available penal law arrest data. There were 483 officers who entered the agency under study in 1987. Of these, 278 officers have at least one penal law arrest available for analysis. The remaining 205 either did not make a penal law arrest during their (presumably short) career (n = 95) or had missing data (n = 110). These analyses, and the similar analyses presented later for the Early 1990s cohort, assume officers are missing penal law arrest data at random.

The mean penal law arrests of the three trajectory groups are compared here to determine if they significantly differ from each other. Secondary arrests, which are suspected to indicate a form of misconduct and are not necessarily be related to productivity levels, are also examined. Thus, if the three trajectory groups significantly differ in their mean arrests, with the high-rate trajectory displaying higher mean arrests, one might suspect that the relationship between membership in a citizen complaint trajectory and the mean uses of force and prevalence of civil litigation is spurious. However, as Terrill and McCluskey (2002) found in their analysis, officers might be both proactive and also problematic, with problem officers producing more arrests, but also engaging most often in coercion. To the extent one finds the high-rate trajectory group to have higher arrest rates, but also higher secondary arrests rates, one might suspect that the high-rate group's career path in misconduct is attributable *to both* arrest activity and misconduct.

The mean arrests and secondary arrests for each citizen complaint trajectory are displayed in Table 5.8. As one can observe from the table, the "good apples" hypothesis does have some support: the high-rate trajectory has the highest mean arrests, while the low-rate trajectory has the lowest arrests, and the mid-rate trajectory falls in between these two groups. A one-way ANOVA shows these differences to be statistically significant using the .10 alpha-level, but the differences in the mean arrests are not large. The low-rate trajectory group averages about 15 arrests per year while the high-rate group averages about 21 per year.[19] It is unlikely that the disparity in both the prevalence of uses of force and civil litigation is solely attributable to the difference in mean arrests between the trajectory groups, but it nevertheless demonstrates that some of the differences in misconduct between the trajectory groups may be attributable to productivity, given there is a 40 percent increase in average arrests between the low- and high-rate trajectories.

Table 5.8 Average Primary & Secondary Arrests by Trajectory for the Late 1980s Cohort

	Low-Rate (n = 137)	Mid-Rate (n = 121)	High-Rate (n = 20)	F-Ratio
Primary Arrest Rate	15.23	16.76	20.82	2.903*
Secondary Arrest Rate	0.70	0.89	1.30	9.037**

* p < .10
** p < .05

---

19. The Dunnett's T3 procedure reveals that only the low- and high-rate trajectories significantly differ in terms of their average primary arrest rates.

Since the high-rate officer group was small and had numerous complaints filed against them, their assignment locations at the times of complaint were extracted from the citizen complaint data file. Examination of assignment reveals little overlap, and certainly no small number of assignments accounts for a disproportionate percentage of where high-rate officers were located. This is not too surprising, given the large number of assignments in the agency under study. What's more, these officers average about 4–5 different assignments over their career based on citizen complaint data, meaning that they managed to obtain complaints across a number of different locations. One might suspect that officers with a proclivity towards deviance would manage to obtain complaints no matter where they find themselves, and perhaps this is partially attributable to what they are doing (e.g., making more arrests) than where they are assigned.

Also observe from the table that secondary arrests behave much the way one would expect if they are to be seen as a measure of misconduct: the high-rate trajectory group displays the highest average secondary arrest totals, while the low-rate trajectory group displays the lowest, and the mid-rate group falls in the middle of these two rates. The difference in the rates is statistically significant using a one-way ANOVA at the conventional .05 alpha-level, and the mean secondary arrests of the high-rate trajectory are nearly twice that of the low-rate trajectory.[20]

From this analysis, it appears that the "good apples" hypothesis does have some support in this cohort, but Terrill and McCluskey's (2002) notion that officers can be both productive *and* problematic might be a more accurate explanation. Officers in the high-rate group did have the highest mean arrests, but the difference in arrests between the trajectories was not large. Add to this the finding that secondary arrests behaved as one would expect if they were an

---

20. The Dunnett's T3 procedure demonstrates that each trajectory is significantly different from each other in terms of their average secondary arrest rates.

indicator of misconduct, and the hypothesis that productive officers are simply more at-risk for misconduct, and hence are not actually more problematic officers, appears to be incomplete. Of course, the stability of these and the other findings above can be examined by considering the Early 1990s Cohort.

Trajectories of Citizen Complaints: Early 1990s Cohort

This section explores the career patterns of citizen complaints for this group of officers, much as was done with the Late 1980s cohort above. The primary purpose for this series of analyses is to compare results across cohorts to assess stability of the results from the late 1980s cohort. Bear in mind, however, that the Early 1990s cohort only has the potential to serve a maximum of 10.5 years, and the majority of officers served less time than this. While there is not agreed upon minimum number of cases or observations years for utilizing the semiparametric, group-based approach, the simple fact is that the more cases or the more number of observation years one has, the greater the likelihood of distinct trajectories emerging. So, if differences in the results between these two cohorts are found, they may be due to the number of cases and observation years between them.

The analyses begin again by determining the optimal number of groups based on citizen complaints for the Early 1990s cohort.[21] A quadratic function was employed here to link experience and misconduct, since the aggregate curve for this cohort displayed an approximately equal rise and fall in citizen complaints per year of

---

21. Analyses were conducted controlling of rank and sick leave usage. None of those analyses or the conclusions drawn from them is significantly different from those presented above, which includes all officers and does not control for rank or sick leave usage.

Table 5.9 BIC Values for Quadratic Estimates for the Early 1990s Cohort

Number of Groups	Quadratic
1	-2777.16
2	-2667.50*
3	-2672.93
*Best fit by BIC criterion	

experience.[22] Table 5.9 presents the BIC values for the cohort, and as can be seen, a two-group model fits the data best.[23]

The model reveals a low- and high-rate officer trajectory, as displayed in Figure 5.2a. Each trajectory's actual and predicted course is displayed in subsequent Figures 5.2b and 5.2c. As can be seen, each group displays a steady rise and fall in terms of citizen complaints, but differing in magnitude. The low-rate group peaks during the fourth year of experience at .18, and the high-rate group peaks during year five at nearly 1.

The parameters estimates for the selected model and AvePP of assignment are displayed in Tables 5.10a and 5.10b. The estimates for the AvePP are quite high at .95 and .85 for the low- and high-rate groups, respectively.

The misconduct career dimensions are displayed in Table 5.11. Again, these trajectory groups behave differently in important, but expected, ways. There were a total of 1,048 citizen complaints filed against officers in this cohort. The low-rate group accounts for the vast majority of officers, and also for a majority of the citizen com-

---

22. As with the previous cohort, iterations employing all possible combinations of intercept-only, linear, quadratic, and cubic polynomials were examined for two to four groups. The quadratic polynomial models performed best in terms of their BIC and AvePP when compared to the other models.

23. Again, as with the Late 1980s cohort, there were no significant differences between year of entry and trajectory group membership.

plaints filed. The high-rate group, by contrast, accounts for about 12 percent of the cohort, but 42 percent of the complaints filed. None of the officers in the low-rate group are labeled as problem

Figure 5.2a Two Group Predicted Trajectory Model for Early 1990s Cohort

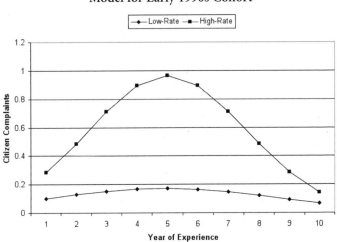

Figure 5.2b Low-Rate Trajectory for Early 1990s Cohort

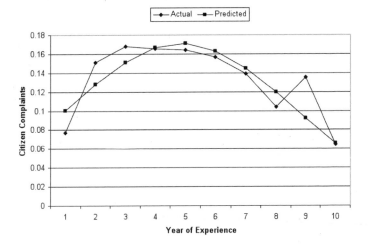

Figure 5.2c High-Rate Trajectory for Early 1990s Cohort

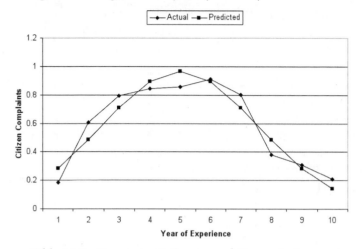

Table 5.10a Parameter Estimates and Group Assignment Probabilities for the Early 1990s Cohort

Group	Parameter	Estimate	SE	T
1	Intercept	-2.612	0.184	-14.227
	Linear	0.349	0.082	4.22
	Quadratic	-0.036	0.008	4.301
2	Intercept	-1.948	0.251	-7.764
	Linear	0.766	0.112	6.828
	Quadratic	-0.077	0.011	-6.784
	BIC = -2667.50 (n = 613)			
Group Membership				
1	(%)	85.182	2.747	31.013
2	(%)	14.818	2.747	5.395

Table 5.10b Posterior Probability Estimates for the Early 1990s Cohort

Groups	Low-Rate	High-Rate
Low-Rate	.95	.15
High-Rate	.05	.85

Table 5.11 Citizen Complaint Trajectories and Misconduct
Elements for Early 1990s Cohort

Variable	Low-Rate (n = 541)	High-Rate (n = 72)
Cohort Member (%)	88.3	11.7
Total number of complaints	603	449
Mean number of complaints	1.1	6.2
Cohort complaints (%)	58	42
Mean year of onset	3.8	2.5
Number of problem officers (6+ citizen complaints)	0	32
Number of active officers	76	74
Mean frequency	.38	.97
Mean career length	4.1	4.4
Mean year of desistance	5.8	5.8

officers. As expected, the high-rate group displays an earlier onset when compared to the low-rate group. Among "active" officers, the high-rate group displays a greater frequency of citizen complaints and also a slightly longer career duration when compared to the low-rate group. There was no difference in the mean year of desistance, but this is likely due to the fewer number of years served during the observation period by officers in this cohort.

Profiles of Citizen Complaint Trajectories: Early 1990s Cohort

The demographic profiles of the citizen complaint trajectories are presented in Table 5.12.[24] Much like the trajectory groups from the

---

24. Again, mean age at entry is not included in these analyses as it did not vary by trajectory group.

Table 5.12 Profiles of Citizen Complaint Trajectories for the
Early 1990s Cohort

Demographic Variables	Low-Rate (n = 541)	High-Rate (n = 72)
Cohort		
% of Population	88.3	11.7
Gender		
Male (%)	85.4	94.4
Female (%)	14.6	5.6
Total	100.0	100.0
Race		
White (%)	86.3	80.6
Black (%)	7.9	16.7
Hispanic (%)	7.6	8.3
Other (%)	.4	1.4
Total	100.0	100.0
Background Characteristics		
Military Service (%)	13.7	19.4
No Military Service (%)	86.3	80.6
Total	100.0	100.0
College Degree (%)	69.9	75.0
No College Degree (%)	30.1	25.0
Total	100.0	100.0

Late 1980s cohort, officers in the high-rate trajectory are more likely to be male, Black, to have served in the military prior to their career as a police officer, and to not have a college degree. However, unlike the previous cohort, high-rate groups were also more likely to be Hispanic or fall into the "Other" category. Why Blacks are the subject of so many citizen complaints remains to be seen, but like the Late 1980s cohort, the arrest rates of Black officers are the lowest when compared to Hispanic and White officers, thus ruling out productivity as a possible explanation.

The results to determine if the two trajectory groups significantly differed from one another in terms of their background and demographic characteristics are presented in Table 5.13.[25] As can be seen from the table, the officers who are male and Black were significantly more likely to be assigned to the high-rate trajectory, which is a replication of the results found in the Late 1980s cohort. Education no longer appears to be a significant protective factor, but this appears likely due to the vast majority of officers in the Early 1990s having a college degree. Since an increasing number of officers are obtaining their degrees, perhaps this indicator loses its ability to detect these traits.

Table 5.13 Demographic Predictors of Citizen Complaint Trajectory Membership for the Early 1990s Cohort

Variable	Coefficient Estimate	Standard Error	*t*-Statistic
High-Rate			
Male	1.75	0.90	1.96*
Black	0.81	0.42	1.94*
Hispanic	0.58	0.49	1.18
Military	0.47	0.37	1.28
Degree	0.09	0.34	0.28
N = 715			
* $t < .05$			
Comparison group is the low-rate trajectory			

Correlates of Citizen Complaint Trajectories for the Early 1990s Cohort

The correlates of civil litigation, uses of force, and arrest productivity are presented for the Early 1990s cohort below. Many of the findings of the Late 1980s cohort are replicated here.

---

25. Since officers in the Other racial category contain so few officers, they are removed from analysis.

Table 5.14 presents the percentage of officers who were ever involved in civil litigation by their trajectory membership. As expected, officers in the high-rate group were significantly more likely to be involved in civil litigation than were officers in the low-rate group.

Table 5.15 presents the average uses of force by trajectory group membership. Only a slight majority of officers, 54.6 percent, used force during the study period for which data are available. Again, the prevalence of force was not equally distributed across the trajectory groups. Here, about one-half of the officers in the low-rate group used force, and about 78 percent of officers in the high-rate group used force. Of those officers using force, the high-rate group employed coercion significantly more times on average than the low-rate group.

Finally, Table 5.16 presents the primary and secondary arrests rates by trajectory group as a means of assessing the "good apples" hypothesis. Again, as with the Late 1980s cohort, officers in the high-rate trajectory had a significantly greater arrest rate than the low-rate trajectory using an alpha-level of .10. In fact, officers in the high-rate group were about 19 percent more productive than the low-rate group. Surprisingly, officers in this cohort did not significantly differ in their rates of secondary arrests. It appears here that the "good apples" hypothesis does have some support in these data, and unlike the Late 1980s cohort, the differences do not relate to secondary arrests.

Table 5.14 Civil Litigation Involvement by Citizen Complaint
Trajectory for the Early 1990s Cohort

Civil Litigation	Low-Rate (n = 541)	High-Rate (n = 72)
No Involvement (%)	81.7	55.6
Involvement (%)	18.3	44.4
Total	100.0	100.0
Chi-Square = 25.849*		
* p < .001		

Table 5.15 Mean Uses of Force by Trajectory for the Early 1990s Cohort

	Trajectory Group		
	Low-Rate (n = 279)	High-Rate (n = 56)	F-Ratio
Mean Uses of Force	2.6	3.5	11.180*

* p < .001

Table 5.16 Average Primary & Secondary Arrests by Trajectory for the Early 1990s Cohort

	Low-Rate (n = 303)	High-Rate (n = 58)	F-Ratio
Primary Arrest Rate	26.69	32.06	3.57*
Secondary Arrest Rate	.29	.30	.011

* p < .10

Comparison of Citizen Complaint Patterns

The difference in citizen complaint patterns between the two cohorts makes for an interesting comparison. While the number of groups present in each cohort is different, research has demonstrated with more data groups can become more finely converged (Eggleston et al., 2004). This appears to be the case with these cohorts. An interesting note is that for the Early 1990s cohort, a three-group model mirroring that of the Late 1980s cohort fit the data reasonably well, except that the low-rate group's AVePP of assignment fell below .70 to .67, and thus this model was not employed. Had data been available for this group for a longer portion of their careers, it is likely that the model fit and AvePPs of assignment would have improved. As it stands, the three-group model for the Early 1990s cohort had too difficult a time discerning between the low- and mid-rate groups.

Even though the number of groups was different, some similar conclusions can be drawn. First, each trajectory displays a single-peaked curve, and the cubic model of the Late 1980s cohort did not display a later upswing after the initial decline. Thus, all officers display a rise in misconduct in the early years of experience and a steady decline thereafter, even for the most problematic, high-rate group. In fact, in the later years of experience, the trajectory groups seem to be engaging in misconduct at similarly low levels. While these peaks varied by trajectory group and by cohort, it can be said that misconduct peaks early (that is, within the first quarter) in officers' careers. This pattern is not likely attributable to promotion, given that results from considering only patrol officers were virtually identical to results considering all officers regardless of rank.

Second, in each cohort emerged a high-rate group that accounted for a disproportionate amount of misconduct. For the Late 1980s cohort, there were two groups who fit this criterion, as both the mid- and high-rate groups accounted for more citizen complaints than the percentage of their cohort membership would lead one to expect. For the Early 1990s cohort, the high-rate group also accounted for a large percentage of the citizen complaint, even though they made up only about 12 percent of the cohort. Also of interest was that the higher-rate groups began their misconduct careers earlier, and thus had a longer duration, than the low-rate groups. The higher-rate groups also had a greater frequency of citizen complaints while active than the low-rate groups.

Conclusion

What do these results imply for police scholars and police administrators? There's certainly welcomed news for the agency at large. First, while most officers will receive complaints in their careers and "offend" in the sense of engaging in some detectable problem behaviors, most will do so at extremely low levels. Given the complexity and difficulty of policing in a democratic society, combined with the difficulty of measuring misconduct through citizen complaints as discussed previously, this overall level is certainly tolerable. Second, officers will decrease their involvement in misconduct over time. Each trajectory displays an early peak, but then a decline in misconduct as experience increases. The mechanism for this decline is unclear, but there is strong support for this pattern over the course of all officer careers. Thus, even high-level "offenders" will eventually curtail their misconduct, which is not predicted by the traditional concept of a problem officer.

Third, given that misconduct seems to peak early in officer careers, it seems that administrators would best focus limited resources for combating misconduct on the first few years of an officer's career. While this finding has been noted in early work on police socialization, given that misconduct is a relatively rare event, having data on when officers are most at-risk for citizen complaints, and thus where to deploy limited resources to combat misconduct, is valuable.

Fourth, high-rate trajectory members seem to have distinguished themselves from the rest of the officers by their fifth year of experience. Such officers are averaging 1 to 1.5 complaints (or more) by that year, which is significantly greater than the other lower-rate trajectories. While it is unlikely that researchers could accurately predict who would and who would not belong to the high-rate trajectory before or during this point, police administrators might be well advised to review officers at this stage of their career to search for differences (perhaps proximal risk factors) that might explain these divergent rates of misconduct. Conversely, the decline in officer misconduct after the sixth year of experience seems to indicate that some scrutiny during this period and shortly thereafter is required to explain the beginning of the desistance process.

With these results one must keep in mind the difficulty in measuring misconduct using citizen complaints. The apparent universal decline over time may be due to officers becoming more skilled at avoiding citizen complaints, or situations in which citizen are likely to complain, without necessarily implying their skill in police-citizen encounters has grown or that routine supervision is having an effect. While the high-rate officers have little overlap in their assignment location based on citizen complaint data, complete career data is lacking on assignment location, and thus it may be that officers who accumulate a significant number of citizen complaints are simply moved indoors, behind a desk, where they are no longer a liability to the agency.

In addition to describing the patterns of misconduct over officer careers, analyses were undertaken to determine what available variables predict these misconduct trajectories. Some of these results support previous research and thinking about misconduct, particularly that males are more likely to engage in misconduct than females, and that education—at least for the Late 1980s cohort—appears to lower the probability of misconduct. This adds further support to the trend of both hiring more female officers and people who have high career expectation in terms of advancement.

Like some previous research concerning problem-officers, Whites were found to be at a lower risk of misconduct than minorities— particularly Black officers. Why this might be the case was discussed previously, but it certainly poses a problem for the agency under study. It is unlikely that minority officers somehow perform less admirably than White officers, but it may be that as the agency is pushed into hiring more minority officers, the pool from which the agency has to draw is limited, so that some minority officers are hired based on racial considerations and not other, more relevant performance criteria. To the extent that this is true, one might expect White officers to perform better than minority officers because of differing standards in terms of entry into the agency.

Another plausible hypothesis is that this variation in misconduct by race is likely attributable to an increased likelihood of a predominately white citizenry to complain against minority officers. This draws attention to a potentially undesirable and unintended consequence of the trend to hire more minority officers, in that such officers in some areas may be more vulnerable to increased numbers of citizen complaints simply due to their minority status. More research is required to further explore this phenomenon, but it does point to a potential problem as police departments nationwide attempt to attract and hire a greater number of Black and Hispanic candidates.

The hypothesis regarding prior military service as a potential risk factor for citizen complaints appears to be unsupported. In the predictive model that included all demographic and background characteristics for both cohorts, prior military service did not predict trajectory group membership. This variable is further explored in the next chapter, as one would expect prior military service to be a significant predictor of citizen complaint trajectories, but not internal complaint trajectories.

The hypothesis regarding education was supported in the Late 1980s Cohort, but not the Early 1990s cohort. For the former cohort, having a degree lowered the probability that an officer would belong to the higher-rate trajectories. For the latter cohort, education was a weak and insignificant predictor of trajectory group membership. The most likely explanation for this finding is that of a period effect — officers in the Early 1990s cohort were much more likely to have a degree than the Late 1980s cohort, so this indicator likely lost its ability to discern highly motivated officers interested in advancing their careers from officers who are less motivated.

This chapter also examined the correlates of involvement in civil litigation and use of force for both cohorts. These variables behaved as expected: those officers who belonged to the high-rate trajectories displayed a greater prevalence of civil litigation and a greater average number of uses of force. Given that some of the variability in these indicators are attributable to misconduct and are not by-products of productivity, this lends support to the validity of the trajectory groups.

As for the "good apples" hypothesis, support is found in both cohorts. Officers in the high-rate group were more likely to have higher rates of primary arrests, even though the differences between the trajectories were not large. This, combined with the findings of secondary arrest rates from the Late 1980s cohort, suggest that while productivity may be partially attributable to citizen complaint totals across officer careers, this is unlikely to be the entire story. It is instead more plausible that high-rate trajectory officers are both productive and problematic, suggesting that while some officers do a large amount of police work, their productivity may be part of a tough and aggressive policing style.

Overall, the analyses presented in this chapter demonstrate that there are multiple pathways of police misconduct, each with their own distinct patterns over time. This is vital in demonstrating that misconduct is not a static phenomenon. While each pathway demonstrates a single peak and a general decline, the timing of the peak and the rate of misconduct over time differs significantly—especially when considering the rarity of citizen complaints against police officers. Moreover, the probability of officer membership in these career pathways differs significantly by several factors. Taken together, these findings highlight important issues in thinking about police misconduct and avenues for its control, which are further discussed in the last chapter.

Chapter 6

Trajectories of
Internal Complaints

Analyses uncovered that the aggregate experience-misconduct curve, as measured by citizen complaints, consists of distinct career pathways which underlie this curve. While the patterns that emerged did not entirely parallel those predicted at the outset of this work, there is evidence supporting the notion that not all officers follow career trajectories in misconduct that match the aggregate experience-misconduct curve.

Attention is now turned towards examining internally-generated complaints. Since no research has been conducted on the frequency or correlates of internal complaints, there are no preliminary hypotheses made up front about the patterns of this complaint type, except that prior military service should not impact trajectory group membership. Still, these complaints merit investigation for a few reasons. First, they are a measure of organizational behavior, and not the behavior of citizens, so they may tell us something about the behavior of officer peers and supervisors. Second, since internal complaints are distinctive indicators from citizen complaints, parceling out these two kinds of complaints may have divergent results. To the extent that this is the case, such results have implications for intervening in police misconduct. Third, even though citizen and internal complaints are different, they may both tap an underlying propensity towards occupational deviance. This chapter examines the intersection of both citizen and internal complaints to determine if officers belonging to one citizen complaint trajectory group are also likely to belong to a particular internal complaint trajectory group. This will, at the very least, enhance the comparisons made among career pathways. It may also shed some light on a measurement issue in police misconduct, and help discern whether citizen and internal complaints both measure the same phenomenon.

Trajectories of Internal Complaints for the Late 1980s Cohort

As with the analyses of citizen complaint trajectories, analyses begin with the Late 1980s cohort, and attempt to discern the optimal number of groups present in the internal complaint data.[1] Also as with the analyses of citizen complaints, a ZIP distribution is employed here, as there are more zeros present than would be expected with the purely Poisson model. A quadratic polynomial is used to link experience and misconduct as measured by internal complaints.[2]

Table 6.1 presents the BIC scores for different numbers of groups. As can be seen, the model improves significantly with the addition of a second group, but the model fit declines with the addition of a third group. A four-group model resulted in false convergence. Thus, the two-group model is selected for internal complaints.

The shapes of the predicted trajectories for both groups are displayed in Figure 6.1a. As can be seen, there exists a low- and high-rate group, but "low-rate" and "high-rate" are relative terms here. Both the trajectories exhibit a very low number of internal complaints, and the high-rate internal complaint trajectory displays numbers similar to the low-rate citizen complaint trajectory. The

---

1. All analyses reported below were done with all officers regardless of rank and with patrol officers only. The results are virtually indistinguishable, so only the results with all officers are reported.

2. As with analyses of citizen complaints, all possible combinations of intercept-only, quadratic, and cubic polynomials were estimated. The quadratic models performed best in terms of their BICs and AvePPs.

Table 6.1 BIC Values for Quadratic Estimates for the Late 1980s Cohort

Number of Groups	Quadratic
1	-3728.45
2	-3682.02*
3	-3687.53
* Best fit by BIC criterion	

actual and predicted paths of both groups are displayed in Figures 6.1b and 6.1c. As with citizen complaint trajectories, discussion will focus upon the predicted trajectories, as these are simpler to discuss due to their smooth course.

As can be seen from the figures, both trajectories are single-peaked, demonstrating a steady rise in the early years of experience and a steady decline thereafter. The largest difference between

Figure 6.1a Two-Group Internal Complaint Model for the Late 1980s Cohort

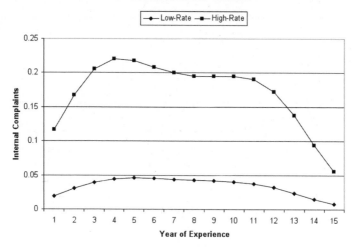

Figure 6.1b Low-Rate Internal Complaint Trajectory

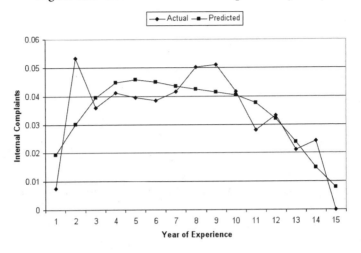

Figure 6.1c High-Rate Internal Complaint Trajectory

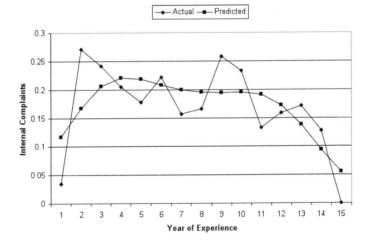

these two trajectories is their magnitude, but again, both exhibit a low number of internal complaints from year-to-year. This is not surprising given that internal complaints make up a very small percentage of personnel complaints.

Table 6.2a displays the parameter estimates for the two group model, and Table 6.2b displays their AvePPs of assignment. As can be seen from the second table, the AvePPs are both greater than .7, but the high-rate group does not exceed .8. These AvePPs are adequate, but the model does struggle somewhat in placing officers in the low- and high-rate group, which might not be surprising given the extremely low numbers of internal complaints overall.

Table 6.3 displays the misconduct career elements of the two trajectories. There were 1,023 internal complaints filed against offi-

Table 6.2a Parameter Estimates and Group Assignment Probabilities for the Late 1980s Cohort

Group	Parameter	Estimate	SE	T
1	Intercept	-4.502	0.364	-12.367
	Linear	0.697	0.111	6.259
	Quadratic	-0.048	0.008	-6.356
2	Intercept	-2.619	0.236	11.079
	Linear	0.597	0.067	8.924
	Quadratic	-0.041	0.005	-8.906
	Alpha0	-3.486	0.713	-4.892
	Alpha1	1.138	0.2	5.696
	Alpha2	-0.075	0.014	-5.428
	BIC = -3682.02 (n = 1138)			
Group Membership				
1	(%)	75.583	5.378	14.054
2	(%)	24.417	5.378	4.54

Table 6.2b Posterior Probability Estimates for the Late 1980s Cohort

Groups	Low-Rate	High-Rate
Low-Rate	.87	.24
High-Rate	.13	.76

Table 6.3 Internal Complaint Trajectories and Misconduct
Elements for Late 1980s Cohort

Variable	Low-Rate (n = 938)	High-Rate (n = 200)
Cohort Member (%)	82.4	17.6
Total number of complaints	402	621
Mean number of complaints	.43	3.1
Cohort complaints (%)	39.3	60.7
Mean year of onset	6.6	4.3

cers in this cohort. The low-rate group comprises the vast majority, 82.4 percent, of the cohort, but accounts for only about 39 percent of all the internal complaints filed. The high-rate group,
conversely, accounts for only 17.6 percent of the cohort, but about
61 percent of the internal complaints filed. So, as with citizen complaints, the internal complaints exhibit a group of officers who account for a small percentage of officers, but a disproportionate
amount of misconduct. Also of note is that the high-rate group, as
one might expect, exhibits an earlier year of onset and a greater
average number of internal complaints than the low-rate group.[3]

Profiles of Internal Complaint
Trajectories for the Late 1980s Cohort

With the number of trajectories decided upon, each cohort member can be assigned to his/her most probable trajectory, and examination can begin of theses two group's profiles. For this analysis,

---

3. There is no comparison made among the misconduct career elements of active officers as was done with citizen complaints, since no officers in the low-rate group were active (i.e., none had three or more
internal complaints filed against them, or two or more if they left before
the observation period ended).

the low-rate trajectory serves as the comparison group. As with profiles of citizen complaint groups, interest lies in comparing the low- and high-rate trajectories to discern what, if any, demographic and background characteristics can distinguish between membership in these two groups. Also, later comparisons of citizen and internal complaint trajectories in the Late 1980s cohort will discern if the high-rate offenders who emerged using citizen complaint data also tend to be the same officers who belong to the high-rate internal complaint trajectory.

Table 6.4 displays the analyses of the demographic profiles of the low- and high-rate groups for internal complaints. As with the analyses of citizen complaints, the high-rate officers here tend to be minority and less educated than low-rate officers. Interestingly, the difference between male and female officers by trajectory group is negligible, as one might anticipate males as more likely to receive internal complaints than females, as was found with citizen complaints. Having prior military experience does not seem to differ between the trajectory groups either, which is expected, as it was hypothesized earlier that military personnel would readily adapt to the paramilitary structure of a police department.

Table 6.5 presents the results from the model statistically testing whether one or more demographic or background characteristics distinguish the probability of group membership across the two trajectory groups. As one can see from the table, minorities (both Blacks and Hispanics) are significantly more likely to belong to the high-rate trajectory, while those officers with a college degree are less likely to belong to this trajectory. As with the citizen complaint trajectories for this cohort, being a minority and not having a college degree sometime during one's career are risk factors for belonging to the high-rate trajectory. Perhaps college educated officers perform not only better in interactions with citizens, but more often meet supervisory expectations as well. This result is still surprising, given that the majority of the research on the educational effects on police officer attitudes and behavior have produced little in the way of detectable effects. However, some research has found that officers with more education are less likely to receive

Table 6.4 Profiles of Internal Complaint Trajectories for the Late 1980s Cohort

Demographic Variables	Low-Rate (n = 938)	High-Rate (n = 200)
Cohort		
% of Population	82.4	17.6
Gender		
Male (%)	90.6	89.0
Female (%)	9.4	11.0
Total	100.0	100.0
Race		
White (%)	77.3	54.0
Black (%)	12.4	33.0
Hispanic (%)	9.8	12.5
Other (%)	0.5	0.5
Total	100.0	100.0
Background Characteristics		
Military Service (%)	91.6	93.0
No Military Service (%)	8.4	7.0
Total	100.0	100.0
College Degree (%)	48.9	64.5
No College Degree (%)	51.1	35.5
Total	100.0	100.0

Table 6.5 Demographic Predictors of Internal Complaint Trajectory Membership for the Late 1980s Cohort

Variable	Coefficient Estimate	Standard Error	t-Statistic
High-Rate			
Male	-0.40	0.43	-0.95
Black	2.08	0.32	6.48*
Hispanic	0.95	0.38	2.51*
Military	-0.44	0.48	-0.94
Degree	1.08	0.29	-3.72*

N = 1132

* t < .05

Comparison group is the low-rate trajectory

citizen complaints and more likely to be praised by supervisors, which may account for these results (Worden, 1990).

Similar to the results of the citizen complaint trajectories, minority officers were more likely to be in the high-rate trajectory. Again, it is not possible to test why this might be the case with these data, although similar hypotheses could be posed as was offered previously for citizen complaints: it could be that either minority officers do not perform as well within the agency as Whites, or that the predominate group of White officers are more likely to complain against minority officers given an observed act of misconduct or violation of departmental policy. Again, these two explanations are also not mutually exclusive.

Comparing Citizen Complaint and Internal Complaint Trajectories for the Late 1980s Cohort

Not only is there interest in whether demographic and background characteristics matter in terms of the likelihood of belonging to one trajectory over another, there is additional interest in how trajectories of both citizen and internal complaints intersect. Table 6.6 presents the cross-tabulation of these two sets of trajectory groups from the Late 1980s cohort, and the chi-square statistic for this table is significant. As can be seen from the table, officers belonging to one low-rate trajectory group will likely belong to the other, and officers belonging to one high-rate trajectory group will likely belong to the other. While most of the citizen complaint trajectories belong to the low-rate internal complaint trajectories, the percentage of officers in the citizen complaint trajectories comprising the low-rate internal group decreases as one moves to the mid- and high-rate groups. Likewise, an increasing percentage of officers in the high-rate internal complaint trajectory comprise the higher-rate citizen complaint trajectories. Thus, it appears that there is some correspondence between citizen and internal complaint trajectories. This indicates that both are measuring an underlying proclivity to engage in problematic behaviors, although the association between these measures is not as strong as one might expect, the Tau-c for Table 6.6 is only .17, indicating a weak association between the trajectory groups.

Table 6.6 Intersections of Internal and Citizen Complaint Trajectories

	Citizen Complaint Trajectory		
Internal Complaint Trajectory	Low-Rate	Mid-Rate	High-Rate
Low-Rate (%)	89.0	75.2	59.0
High-Rate (%)	11.0	24.8	41.0
Chi-Square = 57.53*			
* p < .001			
Tau-c = .17			

Internal Complaint Trajectories: Early 1990s Cohort

Having examined the patterns and profiles of internal complaints for the Late 1990s cohort, it is now time to turn analytic attention to the Early 1990s cohort. Again, as with the previous chapter, this cohort is examined as a means of discovering the stability of the findings from the Late 1980s cohort.

As was done with the previous analyses, one begins by attempting to discern the optimal number of groups underlying the aggregate internal complaint curve. As with the citizen complaint data for this cohort, the Poisson distribution is employed and a quadratic polynomial is used to link experience and misconduct as measured by internal complaints. Table 6.7 displays the BIC scores for vari-

Table 6.7 BIC Values for Quadratic Estimates
for the Early 1990s Cohort

Number of Groups	Quadratic
1	-1132.28
2	-1129.87*
3	-1135.81
* Best fit by BIC criterion	

ous numbers of groups for the model. Unlike previous results, there is not a significant increase in BIC scores from the one- to the two-group model, although there is still an increase. The three-group model decreases the BIC, noting a decline in model fit. Thus, a two-group model would be selected, noting a low- and high-rate group whose behavior patterns are similar to those displayed in Figure 6.1a. However, there are only 21 officers in the high-rate group, a number too small for meaningful analysis. While there is no agreed upon number of minimum cases that are required for a trajectory to be adequate for analytic purposes, having only 21 officers in the high-rate trajectory, and also only a marginal improvement in BIC from a one- to a two-group model, seems to favor a one-group model here. It is likely that having more years of data on this group would increase the number of officers in the high-rate group, but as it stands, the one-group model is the more parsimonious choice. As such, no additional analyses are required of a single-group trajectory model.

Conclusion

To date, no research has examined closely patterns of internally-generated complaints. While there were no hypotheses proposed at the start of this examination except for the one regarding prior military experience, it is interesting to note the similarities between the analytic results obtained from either citizen or internal complaints for the Late 1980s cohort. First, both sets of analyses for this cohort demonstrate multiple trajectories underlying the aggregate experience-misconduct curve based on complaint type. Also, both analyses demonstrate the presence of a low- and high-rate group, and both display similar patterns in terms of the timing of their peaks. While there is certainly a difference in the degree of magnitude between citizen complaint-based trajectories and internal complaint-based trajectories, each are single peaked and that peak occurs early in officer careers.

Additionally, many variables included to predict for trajectory group membership are similar for the Late 1980s cohort. Minority officers are more likely to comprise the high-rate trajectories, and officers who are educated were less likely to belong to the high-rate trajectories based on both citizen and internal complaints.

Prior military experience did not behave as expected. This variable had no impact on the probability of either citizen or internal complaint-based trajectory membership. This indicates that prior military history does not have a differential effect upon trajectory group membership—it is neither a risk nor a protective factor.

Sex was a significant risk factor that differed between the citizen complaint trajectory analyses for the Late 1980s cohort. Females were at a decreased risk of belonging to the high-rate citizen complaint trajectory than males, but this was not true of internal complaints. Sex appears to have no impact on peer's or supervisor's likelihood of filing internal complaints. This is somewhat surprising, given that research has documented male resistance to accepting female officers (Walker, 1985).

The results from the Early 1990s cohort do temper the conclusions one can draw from the analyses of the Late 1980s cohort. Somewhat unexpectedly, the number of trajectories underlying the experience-internal complaint curve did not accord well between the cohorts. Whether this is a substantive finding or an artifact of the varying time period for which data was obtained for each cohort is not known.

From these analyses of internal complaints, it appears that police administrators should be less concerned with the quantity of these types of complaints when compared with citizen complaints, but would nonetheless be advised not to completely ignore them. Officers with high rates of internal complaints were more likely to also accumulate high-rates of citizen complaints (and vice-versa), and to the extent these two are associated, it appears that to some (albeit low) degree they are both measuring the same underlying propensity to engage in problematic behavior. However, since the relationship between these two complaint types is not strong, administrators employing EIS would be advised to either concentrate on citizen complaints, or personnel complaints overall. Parceling out internally-generated complaints as a means of identifying problematic officers would appear to be a less effective effort, given their extremely low rates and weak association to citizen complaints.

Chapter 7

Implications for Policy and Priorities for Research

This work began with the premise that taking a developmental view of police misconduct could improve both theoretical development and policy on this important issue. Specifically, it was argued that concepts from the literature on criminal careers and developmental criminology can be borrowed, with some adaptation, and applied to police as a way to enhance understanding of misconduct. The point of departure for this work began with problem officers, but has attempted to move beyond consideration of this small group by placing them within a larger framework that emphasizes officer behavior over time. As it stands currently, very little research on police considers officers within a career context, and there is no research on individual patterns of police misconduct over time. Thus, this research is primarily exploratory, and examines the patterns of misconduct over the course of officer careers and the correlates of those patterns.

Using data from an Early Intervention System project, this research has examined the misconduct of officers, measured by personnel complaints, from two cohorts. The first cohort began their careers in the years between 1987 and 1990, and the second in the years 1991 and 1994. The study period for observation was 14.5 years, from January 1st, 1987 to June 30th, 2001. While this period does not cover entire officer careers, it does provide a window in which to consider a large section of the first-quarter to first-half (or more) of service. Utilizing this window, and employing analytic strategies developed by criminologists for exploring antisocial behavior over time, the misconduct of officers at both the aggregate and individual level has been examined.

A Brief Review of the Empirical Results

The first research question posed in this work was whether, at the aggregate level, there existed an experience-misconduct curve. It was expected that if such a curve existed, its pattern would display a quick rise and sharp peak in the early years of experience, with a steady decline thereafter. It was also expected that the number of misconduct occurrences, as measured by personnel complaints, would be fairly low across officer careers. Finally, it was expected that while participation would be fairly low, a small percentage of officers would account for a disproportionate amount of misconduct.

Nearly all of these hypotheses regarding the experience-misconduct curve are supported. At the aggregate level, experience and misconduct are related in an orderly way, with misconduct rising sharply and peaking in the early years (within the first five years) of experience, and then steadily declining thereafter. The results were similar whether considering only patrol officers or all officers regardless of rank, and average misconduct totals, even at their peak, were generally low (a rate of less than .35 citizen complaints). This is the first empirical confirmation of this implied relationship between officer experience and officer misconduct in the literature.

Regarding particular misconduct career elements, it was found that participation was high, while frequency was fairly low, which did not meet initial expectations. While in both cohorts it was found that a small percentage of officers (about 10 percent) accounted for a disproportionate amount of citizen complaints (about 30 percent), those officers who had enough citizen complaints to estimate career dimensions of frequency, duration, and desistance tended to be small in number, and moreover, the frequency of problem behaviors while active was very low. Thus, it appears likely that the shape of the experience-misconduct curve was driven primarily by prevalence, with fewer and fewer officers beginning their misconduct careers in the later years of experience, and only committing detectable offenses (in terms of citizen complaints) once or twice, than simply a few officer driving the numbers with long careers and a high frequency of problem behaviors.

Of course, both patterns do exist in the data, so the curve is not entirely created by only participation or only frequency—officers differ in their misconduct *over* experience.

Three citizen complaint trajectories were predicted to underlie the experience-misconduct curve for both cohorts, and while this was found to be the case in the Late 1980s cohort, only one of these trajectories behaved as anticipated. In the Late 1980s cohort, a mid-rate trajectory group that mirrored the experience-misconduct curve was found, and comprised about 36 percent of the cohort. Thus, some officers in this cohort behaved much like the aggregate pattern, although this was not the modal experience.

The other two trajectory groups, uncovered in both cohorts, did not follow the anticipated pathways. First, there was no abstainer group found. Instead, a low-rate trajectory group was found that averaged a near-constant level over their career. This rate was extremely low, never exceeding an average of .2 for either cohort. It is interesting that the low-rate group comprised the majority of the cohorts, as one might anticipate, given the police socialization literature and the pattern of the experience-misconduct curve, that the mid-rate trajectory would compose the modal officer experience over time.

Second, no problem officer trajectory was found. The problem officer concept implies a trajectory where offending would peak early, would be very high, and that high rate would continue across a career barring some intervention or career termination. Such a trajectory was not present. Instead, a high-rate group was found, comprising only a small percentage of both cohorts. This group certainly engages in more frequent misconduct at greater rates when compared to the other trajectories, but this group also displays a single peak with a steady decline thereafter. While this high-rate trajectory has an earlier onset, a later peak, and a higher frequency than the other trajectories, this high-rate trajectory does not maintain its frequency across careers. By the later years of experience, the high-rate group displays average complaint totals similar to those of the other trajectories.

The profiles of trajectory groups were also explored. Based on previous research, one would expect officers who engage in misconduct more frequently to be Black, male, have no college education, and have prior military experience. Also, to the extent that citizen complaints measure misconduct, one would expect these officers to use force more often and be more likely to be involved in civil litigation during their careers.

Partial support is found for the hypothesized profile of the high-rate trajectory group. Officers in the high-rate group in both cohorts were predominately male, more likely to be Black, and those in the Late 1980s cohort were less likely to have a college degree. However, military service had no discernable effect on trajectory membership.

Once officers were sorted into their trajectory groups, it was found that officers in the high-rate trajectory group displayed a larger percentage of prevalence of civil litigation and a greater frequency of uses of force than the other, lower-rate trajectories. Again, data on the use of force and civil litigation was not available for the entire study period, so these correlates could not be examined for each year of experience for all officers in both cohorts. It would have been interesting to examine whether trajectory group membership predicted early onset of force utilization or involvement in civil litigation, or whether trajectory group membership predicted an above average frequency of these correlates over the career course. Nevertheless, to the extent that some of the variation in both civil litigation and uses of force can be attributable to an underlying propensity for problem behaviors, these variables behave as one would predict given misconduct trajectory membership.

Examinations were also undertaken, for a subset of officers, to assess whether misconduct trajectory group predicts primary and secondary arrest totals. One might suspect that officers who are the most proactive would also be the officers most at risk for complaints, uses of force, and the like. As it turns out, some support for this "good apples" hypothesis is found. In both cohorts, officers in the high-rate citizen complaint trajectory had higher average arrests, although this difference was not large. Thus, it was unlikely that productivity is solely driving previous findings regarding the correlates. Moreover, officers in the high-rate trajectory in the Late 1980s cohort were also more likely to have higher averages of secondary arrests, although this finding was not replicated in the Early 1990s cohort.

Finally, there were analyses undertaken of internal complaint trajectories, although no hypotheses were made regarding this complaint type as little research has investigated internal complaints. A two-group trajectory model was found to fit the data for the Late 1980s cohort, with both a low-rate and high-rate trajectory emerging. While the aggregate rates of internal complaints by experience did not produce a distinct pattern as did citizen complaints, the trajectories of internal complaints resembled those of citizen complaints: there was a sharp increase during the first few years of experience, and then a steady decline thereafter. The difference of course was that of magnitude—the amount of misconduct for both the high- and low-rate internal complaint trajectories were much lower than that of the corresponding citizen complaint trajectories. However, when cross-tabulated, officers in the high-rate internal complaint trajectory group were generally more likely to belong to the higher-rate citizen complaint trajectory groups, indicating the two do tend to measure an underlying proclivity towards misconduct, even though the association between these groups was weak.

Overall, these analyses proved fruitful, even though they provide for only a first-step in taking a developmental view of problem behaviors. First, this work provides solid empirical evidence of a long-speculated relationship between experience in police work and problem behaviors. The experience-misconduct curve implied so often in early police research exists, and this relationship has implications for both theoretical advancement and policy regarding misconduct. What's more, distinct pathways of misconduct underlie this curve, and their shape, function, and corresponding profiles, while not entirely predicted by the literature, certainly has implications for police administrators and researchers.

Theoretical Implications

Part of the contribution of this work is in development of theory. It has been argued here that police misconduct — understood as a special set of antisocial behaviors — can be framed in terms of a "career" from a developmental perspective. Such a framework advances both criminological theory and theory of police behavior.

For criminology, this research can be seen as a logical extension of developmental criminology, broadening its consideration to antisocial behaviors during employment. While most thinking in criminology views legitimate employment as an important life event that should decrease antisocial behavior because of its value in increasing one's stake in conformity, net of any underlying propensity to offend, it can be argued that not all employment opportunities may be beneficial. When applying this framework to police, one must consider its unique occupational characteristics — namely that police in the United States are socialized into a distinct subculture, operate with little direct supervision, and are the only occupation in the country with the capacity to legitimately employ coercive force on citizens. Thus, one might theorize that candidates with an underlying propensity to engage in antisocial behavior might display those tendencies on the job because of occupational characteristics associated with the police role. In short, policing provides a unique opportunity for deviance that one does not encounter in many other occupations. An individual who has a propensity towards antisocial behavior that has not made manifest of that tendency due to protective factors, or other events that limit opportunity, may suddenly manifest those tendencies because of the structural characteristics of policing. In this sense, police misconduct could be seen in criminological terms as a special case of adult onset, a topic with very little coverage in the literature.

To the extent that developmentally-derived hypotheses hold true when considering a form of occupational deviance—namely police misconduct—one could argue that such ideas can be broadened beyond just consideration of crime across age to consideration of occupational deviance across experience in various occupations. This would expand the generalizability of these concepts, and one could even hypothesize further extensions of this theory and related concepts to other occupations within the criminal justice system (e.g., lawyers, corrections officers) or other employment opportunities (e.g., medical doctors engaging in malpractice).

The other theoretical contribution of this work is to advance thinking about police behavior by adopting a developmental perspective. Precious little research considers any police behavior over time, and such work has focused (understandably) on the first year of officer careers. Moreover, little thinking has been done which considers changes within officers over their career course, even though frequently the amount of time on the job has been thought to impact a wide range of police attitudes and behaviors. Thus, many theories and hypotheses of police behavior are static and do not consider the interplay of underlying antisocial propensity and career events over time. There is much potential for theoretical gain by considering within-officer changes in behavior over time, and future police research should begin moving in this direction where possible.

Policy Implications

The finding likely to be of most interest to police administrators is the shape of the trajectories, and their similarity to the overall shape of the aggregate experience-misconduct curve. Because it appears that all officers who engage in problem behaviors do so early (recall onset was during the third year of experience), and the peak comes in about the fifth or sixth year of experience with a steady decline thereafter, the only true concern is the magnitude of problem behaviors within this general trend. In other words, while some officers certainly engage in deviance earlier and more often than others, even the high-rate officers desist over time. Thus, the main focus on administrative intervention for misconduct should be between the first and fifth year (or so) of experience, as this is the point at which officers diverge from the modal pattern.[1] The question of course becomes one of identifying the higher-rate officers from the lower-rate officers. Since current research on problem officers, and interventions such as EIS designed to combat their behaviors, captures officers when the experience-misconduct curve is at its peak, it is difficult to say whether any particular officer will belong to a high-rate trajectory in the future.

Here is another example of where the analogy employed in this research to developmental criminology is advantageous. Criminologists have been concerned with identifying career criminals for quite some time, but have had virtually no success in doing so. Thus, researchers have instead abandoned the notion of prospective identification of offenders and instead have focused on risk factors and protective factors related to antisocial behavior. As noted earlier, the risk factor prevention paradigm has gained considerable currency in criminology and has allowed both researchers and practitioners to have a dialogue about how best to go about preventing future antisocial behavior (typically delinquency) by reducing known risk factors and enhancing known protective factors. Thus, research has focused on whether certain risk factors from domains such the school, family, peer group, community, and the individual affect the likelihood of later offending. Protective factors have generally fallen into 3 basic categories: individual characteristics, social bonding, and healthy beliefs (Pollard et al., 1999).

---

1. It should be noted that the data does not allow exploration of officers at the end of their career. One might speculate that officers (especially patrol officers) who are approaching retirement might engage in more frequent problem behaviors once they reach the point where their pensions cannot be taken away from them and thus have less of a stake in their future.

Some findings regarding this research are important for the current discussion. First, some risk factors, which have been consistently linked with delinquency across varying samples in different countries, have been know to have multiplicative effects (Herrenkohl et al., 2000). Thus, some youth exposed to several risk factors may be much more likely to commit a crime than youth exposed to only one or two. Moreover, when or during what period a youth is exposed to a specific risk factor is important in considering what effects it will have, thus emphasizing the point that interventions must be tailored to a specific stage of development. Finally, even though risk factors may be employed to detect the likelihood of later offending, criminologists are often confronted with a tremendous conundrum: many youth with multiple risk factors never commit a crime. This has led criminologists to seek what are termed *mediator variables* that lie in-between and can account for much of the relationship between risk factors and antisocial behavior. For example, attitudes toward drug use might mediate the relationship between peer and individual drug use. This has also led criminologists to explore the concept of *resilience,* or how protective factors might directly oppose risk factors (an additive model) or buffer against their negative effects (an interactive model) (Pollard et al., 1999). As it stands, there is some debate ongoing among those involved with delinquency prevention as to whether intervention efforts should only focus on the enhancement of protective factors, thus targeting only strengths and thus positive outcomes, or whether a strategy containing consideration of risk factors is more appropriate.

For those familiar with the policing literature on accountability, the parallels here are stark and exciting. Currently, police departments attempt to curtail potential future deviance through screening methods and monitoring of problem behavior. As stated previously, it is likely that screening only eliminates only the most extreme candidates in terms of deviance, and many departments, either because of too few applicants or pressure to hire more diverse officers, have lowered their hiring standards. Thus, it has become increasingly important to monitor officer behavior while on-the-job, and the increasingly dominant technology for doing so is through EIS. Yet these systems are very rudimentary, relying on administrators to intuitively set thresholds for when an officer becomes a "problem" worthy of intervention. Borrowing from criminology, administrators could focus more efforts on understanding various risk factors for misconduct across a variety of domains that are currently not considered, how multiple risk factors may place officers at increased risk of misconduct, and how certain risk factors occurring at certain times in officer careers may play a role in assessing future misconduct. Moreover, one could also explore protective factors and their role in increasing resilience of officers from engaging in misconduct. Knowledge of risk and protective factors, and how they contribute to misconduct, would contribute to police accountability by both enhancing the predictive validity of EIS and by allowing departments to tailor interventions in such a way as to minimize risk factors and enhance protective factors. Also, since misconduct is relatively infrequent, especially when measuring this concept with personnel complaints, knowing something about risk factors, protective factors, and multiple correlates of police misconduct adds more data with which to triangulate the location of officers who are most at-risk for problem behaviors in a police population.

Some of the research here begins to identify factors related to the risk factor prevention paradigm. Analyses of demographic and background factors were conducted with a view towards identifying characteristics associated with membership in each trajectory, and finds that males and minorities are most at-risk for problem behaviors. Being female and having a college education was also found to lower this risk. Additionally, when examining career elements, officers with an earlier onset of problem behaviors had a higher frequency and longer duration than officers with later onset times. This suggests that, of those who deviate, early onset places officers at risk for repeated, and prolonged bouts of problem behaviors. While these analyses were a rudimentary first-cut, they nevertheless suggest that there are risk and protective factors that can be utilized by administrators, and it is likely many more exist.

Research Implications

Another contribution of this work is its implications for police scholars. First, as the EIS Project demonstrates, data can be collected on officers over their career course. As agencies adopt and implement EIS, numerous indictors of problem behaviors will be available, in computerized form, which will be a boon to scholars who are interested in taking a career view of police officer behavior, provided they can obtain access to them.

Second, the shape of the experience-misconduct curve and their underlying trajectories has implications for police intervention efforts. If problem behaviors generally decline over time after their initial peak, any consideration of an intervention's effect on problem behaviors must take into account the general shape of the aggregate curve. Even in the absence of an intervention it appears the stability of police deviance is not constant, and thus intervention evaluations must be concerned with when the intervention occurs in an officer's career, and also whether it is a given intervention or the decline in problem behaviors more generally that is having an effect on officer behavior. In short, one does not wish to attribute a decline in problem behaviors on a particular intervention if such behaviors would have declined even without an intervention.

Third, it appears that citizen and internal complaint trajectories do have some degree of association, suggesting that the two both measure an underlying propensity towards deviance. However, the degree of association between these two are not as strong as one would like, implying that variation in these measures are also attributable to other causes. One such cause may be, as the "good apples" hypothesis suggests, arrest productivity. Officers in the higher-rate citizen complaint trajectories did have higher mean arrest rates, and as such citizen complaints may be related to productivity. Secondary arrests, at least for the Late 1980s cohort, also found that officers in the higher-rate citizen complaint trajectories have higher mean secondary arrest rates, suggesting that such officer may use questionable cover charges to conceal their misconduct. As such, any analysis of citizen complaints must take arrest productivity into account, as variation in citizen complaints appear to be partially attributable to proactive police work, but it also appears likely that proactive officers are both productive and problematic. This poses a challenge to researchers in that data needs to be sufficiently detailed so that one can separate productive officers who receive illegitimate complaints from productive officers who engage in problem behaviors and use arrests to protect themselves from scrutiny.

Fourth, while controls for arrest productivity appear important, controls for exposure time such as rank and sick leave did not have a significant effect on the results. Perhaps this is not surprising in that officers used very little sick leave across their career course, with the vast majority of officers not using any leave. Promotion was also not common, and few officers were promoted early in their careers. Thus, officers who were promoted were already in their career phase when their problem behaviors were on the decline or had reached their low point.

Before concluding this section, a few caveats are in order. First, measuring misconduct primarily through citizen complaints brings forth a number of drawbacks. The fact that even the effective delivery of police services might lead to a citizen complaint makes the validity of this indicator questionable. Given that the low-rate citizen complaint trajectory never exceeds a rate of .2, one might suspect that this trajectory is largely a reflection of unmerited complaints by citizens against officers, and hence is driven by measurement error. Given that the vast majority of officers in this trajectory have zero, or only one, citizen complaint, this explanation may be all that is required. Of course, given that a large number of problem behaviors go undiscovered, and that even when citizens complain there is no guarantee it will end up in administrative records, one cannot be sure whether this low-rate trajectory would be found, or even if indeed others would be discovered, if every act of misconduct was properly recorded.

Second, using citizen complaints also poses several specific problems when examining police misconduct over time. It was argued previously that one can become more certain about the existence of problem officers when one sees consistent misconduct over the course of an officer's career. This is an advantage over cross-sectional research in that officer heterogeneity is not a concern, but when examining officer behavior using citizen complaints, one must also be cognizant of other, alternative explanations. For example, the results indicate at both the aggregate and individual level, police misconduct, even for the high-rate officers, declines over time. Based on the notion that police officers should mature and gain in skill over time, this would be expected, especially if one had a highly valid and reliable indicator of misconduct. However, when using citizen complaints to measure misconduct, one must also consider the alternative hypothesis that this universal decline might be attributable not to some maturation effect, but instead could imply that officers simply get better at avoiding citizen complaints over time. That is, officers do not necessarily decline in their rates of misconduct over time, but instead simply decline in their rates of detection by citizens, or simply learn, for example, what citizens can be targets of disrespect or such without a likelihood of complaint. The data provide no means by which to examine these competing explanations, and it may be that both are correct.

There is also the concern over exactly what citizen complaints tell researchers. Just as early criminologists were concerned with using arrest data to measure crime, so too must police researchers be concerned with using citizen complaints to measure misconduct. The analogy is very appropriate: concern with arrest records lies in the idea that they tell one more about who the police are likely to arrest rather than any objective measure of criminal activity; concern with citizen complaints lies in the idea that they tell one more about who citizen are likely to complain against rather than any objective measure of misconduct. This is the likely explanation as to why minorities, particularly Blacks, were found to be at-risk for membership in the higher-rate complaint trajectories. While attempts to minimize these threats were undertaken by examining other activities such as productivity, secondary arrests, uses of force, and civil litigation to help validate the misconduct trajectories, one must still be concerned with using citizen complaints as the dependent variable.

There is also one final lesson from criminology that pertains to using citizen complaints to measure misconduct. When developmental criminologists use the concept of continuity to discuss the stability of antisocial behavior across the life course, they are usually not talking about the same behavior. In fact, the concept of antisocial behavior is broad so that varying manifestations can be considered across the life course: temper-tantrums at age 3, fighting with peers at age 7, shoplifting at age 15, illegal drug use at age 19, etc. within the same individual points to continuity of antisocial behavior. Thus, the drop-off one sees in the trajectories of misconduct may be due to the fact that personnel complaints capture a narrow range of antisocial behaviors, the expression of which may change over the course of officer careers. Thus, officers in their early years may be proactive and tend to rely on their authority, thus earning the ire of citizens who complain, but perhaps later in their career officers curtail this behavior, and instead manifest other antisocial behaviors not typically covered by citizen complaints (e.g., engaging in avoidant behavior, such as abusing sick leave). Such alternative behaviors might be captured in internal complaints, but officers are not likely to file such complaints against their peers, or even their subordinates.

A final caveat—while this research could examine a number of demographic and background characteristics as well as the correlates of involvement in civil litigation, uses of force, and productivity, there are a number of variables that ideally should have been included, but were not available. Most importantly, there was limited examination of the contribution of patrol location on misconduct. One would expect that some assignments carry with them an increased probability of police-citizen contact, either because some assignments experience a high crime rate and/or a high volume of calls for service, or that this would result in a greater likelihood of citizen complaints, uses of force, and penal law arrests, regardless of an officer's proclivity towards misconduct. Not being able to examine an officer's assignment leaves the results vulnerable to the alternative explanation that this variable is driving some of the relationships found. Examining the patrol locations of officers in the high-rate group, while not a complete picture of their assignment history, did demonstrate that they serve a variety of assignments during their careers while still managing to accumulate complaints. No small group of assignments accounted for high-rate officers' locations, and there was little overlap in assignment, most likely due to the large number of assignments available in this agency. However, high-rate officers, all of which will eventually draw administrative attention to themselves, may be placed inside a station house where they will have minimal contact with citizens, but this information is not available in the assignment data. Thus, the apparent desistance of the high-rate officers later in their careers may not be one of self-correction, but simply one of opportunity to get into trouble.

Future Research

Given that this research was exploratory, there is a large amount of room for future research, the first and most important of which is replication. It is vital that the existence of the experience-misconduct curve be explored in different police settings. While it is expected that the measure of central tendency, dispersion, skewness, and the like will be somewhat different, it would prove valuable to know whether the overall shape and conclusions drawn from the experience-misconduct curve holds across police departments. The age-crime curve has been one of the most stable relationships in criminology to date, and based on the police literature, the relationship between experience and misconduct (and perhaps some other activities like arrest productivity) might prove very stable as well.

Also very important is replication of the trajectories which underlie the experience misconduct curve. Both cohorts displayed multiple and distinct trajectories of citizen complaints, but the final decision on the ideal number of groups was not definitive (nor has it been in criminological research). Also, the number of internal complaint trajectories was different for each cohort, and it was un-

certain whether there existed even more than one trajectory underlying this complaint type. Examining other complaint data on officers over time would prove valuable in replicating these findings.
Second, one would desire additional data that would shed light
on the risk factors that correlate with, and mechanisms that ultimately underlie, these different trajectory patterns or contribute
to their membership. Such research is desperately needed for informed theory and policy. While trajectories are just approximations
of reality, they nevertheless point toward some understanding of
the magnitude and timing of different offense pathways. Thus, one
would desire data which would allow one to test hypotheses about
why misconduct peaks early, and why all misconduct trajectories decline over time and around the same time (after the sixth year of
experience). Is it that officers mature and grow in skill, therefore
performing better over time? Is it that officers develop increasing
stakes in conformity over time by getting married, having children,
buying a house, etc.? Or is it simply that officers manifest other antisocial tendencies that are not captured with personnel complaints,
without denoting a change in underlying proclivity to engage in
deviance? One would also desire data on variables believed to increase membership in one particular trajectory over another. For
example, one might speculate on both risk factors for increasing
misconduct (e.g., a high degree of impulsivity) and protective factors thought to decrease misconduct (e.g., in-service training or
closer supervision). Future research should explore these mechanisms for the shape of the trajectories and factors that might be
correlated with their membership.

Related to capturing more longitudinal data, some knowledge on
attrition from agencies would be valuable. Some officers only serve
a limited number of years, but there is very little research on why
some officers either (a) never make it through the academy or (b)
never make it past the first few years of experience. Knowledge of
attrition is important in that it is likely not random. That is, the officers with the most serious antisocial tendencies or problems may
be the most likely to drop-out or be terminated. Some research
however has examined involuntary separations from police agen-

cies, which from a risk factor prevention paradigm standpoint is valuable for determining who might be ask risk for career-ending misconduct. Along similar lines, it would be valuable to have knowledge regarding pathways of assignment change and promotion through agencies. Thus, one could examine factors and correlates that determine who gets the most coveted assignments or who gets promoted more quickly, assuming these officers are the ones who perform the best, and examine the personnel complaint history of these officers.

Also of value would be some knowledge of the deterrent impact of sanctions on misconduct. Work is needed to determine if varying punishments of officers have differential effects in terms of misconduct career elements and if these relationships vary by sex, race, etc. It would also be interesting to examine periods between complaints as "recidivism" probabilities, as has been done in the criminological literature, and examine if and how these probabilities are (or are not) conditioned by different sanctions.

Future research should also explore means for obtaining more reliable and valid measures of misconduct over an officer's career. While certainly observational research for prolonged periods of time on a large number of officers is impractical, other research methods designed to capture misconduct might be examined. For example, criminologists have used retrospective self-reports of criminal behavior as a way of examining short-term impacts on criminal careers. This method could be tried with police officers as a means of soliciting them to report on their own misconduct. While it may seem unlikely that officers would not report on such behaviors, the fact that this research largely examines forms of misconduct that may not be particularly egregious, (e.g., verbal harassment) as opposed to career-ending misconduct (e.g., selling narcotics), may prove innocuous enough to merit honest officer responses. Remember that for a long time criminologists assumed offenders would be very unlikely to report on past crimes, especially very serious ones such as robbery and the like, until they began asking them, with (what was then) surprising results. Self-reported police misconduct may operate similarly.

If such efforts prove fruitless, perhaps obtaining better estimates of q, or the probability of a complaint per act of misconduct, would enhance misconduct measurements. Knowing if certain specific acts of misconduct carry with it a greater likelihood of a complaint allows us to know if certain officer types might be over or underrepresented in complaint data. Also knowing if a greater frequency of misconduct results in an increase or decrease in q would be valuable, especially since an increasing frequency with a corresponding decrease in q would imply some form of "learning" effect by which high-rate officers avoid detection (Piquero et al., 2003). Similarly, it would be interesting to explore if certain assignments carry a correspondingly different q, and the extent to which promotion to varying ranks also changes the value of q.

As a final and somewhat parenthetical side note, researchers may also want to explore the extent to which high-rate "offenders" exist in other occupations, in criminal justice or elsewhere. The idea that a small number of persons might be responsible for a large amount of antisocial behavior may not just be limited to criminals and cops. Perhaps this is a phenomenon common to many occupations, similar to the finding in social psychology that in many work groups a small number of people are responsible for a large proportion of the work that gets done (Adams, 1999).

Conclusion

Bridging criminology and criminal justice would often seem unnecessary, if not inappropriate. But at the same time, there are certain circumstances where knowledge and research from one can contribute to advancements in the other. This is one such case. In this research, a criminological framework normally reserved for criminals was utilized and applied to police. It should be noted that while police and criminals should not be considered the same, certainly both can be examined in terms of the antisocial behavior in which they engage over time. Police research has come a tremendous distance since the "research revolution" of the 1970s, but thinking about police misconduct can move some steps further by borrowing lessons learned from criminology.

Both research on criminal activity and research on police misconduct appear to demonstrate the presence of a high-rate offender who is responsible for a disproportionate amount of antisocial behavior: criminologists calls these offenders "career criminals" while police researchers call these offenders "problem officers." While criminologists have progressed by not only conducting empirical research on these career criminals, they have also advanced their thinking by placing these and other criminals in a larger framework that considers criminal careers. Research on problem officers has not yet advanced in this manner, and currently only examines cross-sectional patterns of problem officers. This work argues that a similar line should be taken—that problem officers, as well as other types of police officers, should be understood within a larger framework that considers officer careers. The research here is a small step in that direction, and it considers patterns of police misconduct over a portion of officer careers. The results have been intriguing, and suggest that, at the very least, there is potential in taking a developmental view of police behavior. Of course, there will be tremendous challenges in attempting to gather data on police officers over sufficient parts of their career in order to explore developmental theories of police behavior, but criminologists have already demonstrated that such longitudinal data can be gathered on such difficult, and not to mention transient, populations as those at high-risk of criminal behavior.

Bibliography

Adams, K. (1999). What we know about police use of force. In *Use of Force by Police: Overview of National and Local Data*. Washington, DC: National Institute of Justice, Research Report.

Alpert, G. P. (1989). Police use of deadly force: The Miami experience. In R. G. Dunham & G. P. Alpert (Eds.), *Critical Issues in Policing: Contemporary Readings* (pp. 480–497). Prospect Heights, IL: Waveland Press.

Bahn, C. (1984). Police socialization in the eighties: Strains in the forging of an occupational identity. *Journal of Police Science and Administration*, 12, 390–394.

Barnett, A., Blumstein, A., & Farrington, D. P. (1987). Probabilistic models of youthful criminal careers. *Criminology*, 25, 83–107.

Barnett, A., Blumstein, A., Cohen, J., & Farrington, D. P. (1992). Not all criminal career models are equally valid. *Criminology*, 30, 133–155.

Bayley, D.H. (2002). Law enforcement and the rule of law: Is there a tradeoff? *Criminology & Public Policy*, 2, 133–154.

Bayley, D.H., & Bittner, E. (1984). Learning the skills of policing. *Law and Contemporary Problems*, 47, 35–60.

Bayley, D. H., & Garafalo, J. (1989). The management of violence by police patrol officers. *Criminology*, 27, 1–25.

Balyley, P.H., & Mendelsohn, H. (1969). *Minorities and the police*. New York: Free Press.

Bazley, T.D., Mieczkowski, T., & Lersch, K.M. (2009). Early intervention program criteria: Evaluating officer use of force. *Justice Quarterly*, 26, 107–124.

Bennett, R.R. (1984). Becoming blue: A longitudinal study of police recruit occupational socialization. *Journal of Police Science and Administration, 12,* 47–58.

Black, D., & Reiss, A.J. Jr. (1967). Patterns of behavior in police and citizen transactions. *In Studies of Crime and Law Enforcement in Major Metropolitan Areas,* Vol 2. Report to the President's Commission on Law Enforcement and the Administration of Justice. Washington DC: U.S. Government Printing Office.

Blumstein, A., & Cohen, J. (1979). Estimations of individual crime rates from arrest records. *Journal of Criminal Law & Criminology, 70,* 561–585.

Blumstein, A., Cohen, J., Roth, J.A., & Visher, C. A. (1986). *Criminal careers and "career criminals."* Washington, DC: National Academy Press.

Blumstein, A., Farrington, D.P., & Moitra, S. (1985). Delinquency careers: Innocents, desisters, and persisters. In M. Tonry & N. Morris (Eds.), *Crime and justice: An annual review of research* (Vol. 6, pp. 187–219). Chicago: University of Chicago Press.

Brandl, Steven G., Stroshine, M.S., & Frank, J. (2001). Who are the complaint-prone officers? An examination of the relationship between police officers' attributes, arrest activity, assignment, and citizens' complaints about excessive force. *Journal of Criminal Justice, 29,* 521–529.

Brown, M.K. (1981). *Working the Street: Police Discretion and Dilemmas of Reform.* New York: Russell Sage.

Chevigny, P. (1995). *Edge of the Knife.* New York: The New York Press.

Cohen, B., & Chaiken, J.M. (1972). *Police Background Characteristics and Performance.* New York: Rand Corporation.

Crank, J.P. (1993). Legalistic and order-maintenance behaviors among police patrol officers: A survey of eight municipal police agencies. *American Journal of Police, 12,* 103–126.

Elder, G.H. (1985). Perspectives on the life course. In G. Elder (Ed.), *Life Course Dynamics.* Ithaca, NY: Cornell University Press.

Engel, R.S., Sobol, J.J., & Worden, R.E. (2000). Further exploration of the demeanor hypothesis: The interaction effects of suspects' characteristics and demeanor on police behavior. *Justice Quarterly, 17,* 235–258.

Farrington, D.P. (1986). Age and Crime. In M. Tonry and N. Morris (Eds.), *Crime and justice: An annual review of research* (vol 7). Chicago: University of Chicago Press.

Farrington, D.P. (2000). Explaining and preventing crime: The globalization of knowledge—The American Society of Criminology 1999 presidential address. *Criminology, 38,* 1–24.

Fielding, N.G. (1988). *Joining Forces: Police Training, Socialization, & Occupational Competence.* New York, NY: Routledge, Chapman, & Hall, Inc.

Friedrich, R.J. (1977). *The Impact of Organizational, Individual, and Situational Factors on Police Behavior.* Unpublished doctoral dissertation, University of Michigan.

Friedrich, R.J. (1980). Police use of force: Individuals, situations, and organizations. *Annals of the American Academy of Political and Social Science, 452,* 82–97.

Fyfe, J.J. (1996). Methodology, substance, and demeanor in police observational research: A response to Lundman and others. *Journal of Research in Crime and Delinquency, 33,* 337–348.

Fyfe, J.J., Jones, P.R., Kane, R., & Silver, C. (2002). Bad cops: A study of career-ending misconduct among New York City police officers. Presented at the annual meeting of the American Society of Criminology, Chicago, IL.

Gottfredson, M.R., & Hirschi, T. (1986). The true value of lambda would appear to be zero: An essay on career criminals, criminal careers, selective incapacitation, cohort studies, and related topics. *Criminology, 24,* 213–233.

Gottfredson, M.R., & Hirschi, T. (1988). Science, public policy, and the criminal career paradigm. *Criminology, 26,* 37–55.

Griswold, D.B. (1994). Complaints against the police: Predicting dispositions. *Journal of Criminal Justice, 22,* 215–221.

Hagan, J., & Palloni, A. (1988). Crimes as social events in the life course: Reconceiving a criminological controversy. *Criminology, 26,* 87–100.

Harris, C.J. (2009). Police use of improper force: A systematic review of the evidence. *Victims & Offenders, 4, 1, 25–41.*

Herrenkohl, T.I., Maguin, E., Hill, K.G., Hawkins, J.D., Abbott, R.D., & Catalano, R. (2000). Developmental risk factors for youth violence. *Journal of Adolescent Health, 26, 176–186.*

Hirschi, T. & Gottfredson, M.R. (1983). Age and the explanation of crime. *American Journal of Sociology, 89, 552–584.*

Hirschi, T., & Gottfredson, M.R. (1986). Age and the explanation of crime. In T. Hartnagel and R. Silverman (Eds.), *Critique and Explanation: Essays in honor of Gwynne Nettler.* New Brunswick, NJ: Transaction Books.

Hopper, M. (1977). Becoming a policeman: Socialization of cadets in a police academy. *Urban Life, 6, 149–170.*

Horney, J., Osgood, D.W., & Marshall, I.H. (1995). Criminal careers in the short-term: Intra-individual variability in crime and its relation to local life circumstances. *American Sociological Review, 60, 655–673.*

Huizinga, D., Esbensen, F., & Weiher, A.W. (1991). Are there multiple paths to delinquency? *The Journal of Criminal Law & Criminology, 82, 83–105.*

Hunt, J. (1985). Police accounts of normal force. *Urban Life, 13, 315–341.*

Independent Commission on the Los Angeles Police Department (1991). *Report of the Independent Commission on the Los Angeles Police Department.* Lost Angeles: Independent Commission on the Los Angeles Police Department

Jerglum-Bartusch, D.R., Lynam, D.R., Moffitt, T.E., & Silva, P.A. (1997). Is age important? A general versus developmental theory of antisocial behavior. *Criminology, 35, 13–47.*

Kane, R. (2002). The Ecology of Police Misconduct. *Criminology, 40, 867–896.*

Kappeler, V.E., Sluder, R.D., & Alpert, G.P. (1994). *Forces of deviance: Understanding the dark side of policing.* Prospect Heights, IL: Waveland Press.

Klinger, D.A. (1994). Demeanor or crime? Why "hostile" citizens are more likely to be arrested. *Criminology, 32, 475–493.*

Land, K.C., McCall, P.L., & Nagin, D. (1996). A comparison of Poisson, negative binomial, and semiparametric mixed Poisson regression models. *Sociological Methods & Research, 24,* 387–442.

Laub, J.H., & Sampson, R.J. (1998). The long-term reach of adolescent competence: Socioeconomic achievement in the lives of disadvantaged men. In A. Colby and J. James (Eds.), *Competence and Character Through Life.* Chicago: University of Chicago Press.

Lersch, K.M. (2002). Are citizen complaints just another measure of officer productivity? An analysis of citizen complaints and officer activity measures. *Police Practice and Research, 3,* 135–147.

Lersch, K.M., & Mieczkowski, T. (1996). Who are the problem-prone officers? An analysis of citizen complaints. *American Journal of Police, 15,* 23–44.

Liderbach, J., Boyd, L.M., Taylor, R.W., & Kawucha, S.K. (2007). Is it an inside job? An examination of internal affairs complaint investigation files and the production of nonsustained findings. *Criminal Justice Policy Review, 18,* 353–377.

Loeber, R. (1990). Development and risk factors of juvenile antisocial behavior and delinquency. *Clinical Psychology Review, 10,* 1–41.

Mastrofski, S.D., Reisig, M.D., & McCluskey, J.D. (2002). Police disrespect towards the public: An encounter based analysis. *Criminology, 3,* 519–552.

McElvain, J.P., & Kposowa, A.J. (2004). Police officer characteristics and internal affairs investigations for use of force allegations. *Journal of Criminal Justice, 32,* 265–279.

McNamara, J. (1967). Uncertainties in police work: The relevance of police recruits' background and training. In D.J. Bordua (Ed.), *The Police: Six Sociological Essays.* New York: John Wiley.

Meredith, N. (1984). Attacking the roots of police violence. *Psychology Today, 18,* 20–26.

Moffit, T.E. (1993). Adolescent-limited and life-course-persistent antisocial behavior: A developmental taxonomy. *Psychological Review, 100,* 674–701.

Moskos, P. (2008). *Cop in the Hood*. Princeton, MA: Princeton University Press.

Nagin, D. (1999). Analyzing developmental trajectories: A semi-parametric, group-based approach. *Psychological Methods, 4,* 139–157.

Nagin, D., & Farrington, D.P. (1992a). The stability of criminal potential from childhood to adulthood. *Criminology, 30,* 235–260.

Nagin, D., & Farrington, D.P. (1992b). The onset and persistence of offending. *Criminology, 30,* 501–523.

Nagin, D., & Land, C.L. (1993). Age, criminal careers, and population heterogeneity: Specification and estimation of a nonparametric, mixed Poisson model. *Criminology, 31,* 327–362.

Nagin, D., & Paternoster, R. (1991). On the relationship of past to future participation in Delinquency. *Criminology, 29,* 163–189.

Nagin, D., & Paternoster, R. (2000). Population heterogeneity and state dependence: State of the evidence and directions for future research. *Journal of Quantitative Criminology, 16,* 117–144.

Niederhoffer, A. (1967). *Behind the Shield: The Police in Urban Society*. Garden City, NY: Doubleday & Company, Inc.

Paternoster, R., & Brame, R. (1997). Multiple routes to delinquency? A test of developmental and general theories of crime. *Criminology, 35,* 49–80.

Paternoster, R., Dean C. W., Piquero, A., Mazerolle, P., & Brame, R. (1997). Generality, continuity, and change in offending. *Journal of Quantitative Criminology, 13,* 231–266.

Paternoster, R., & Tripplet, R. (1988). Disaggregating self-reported delinquency and its implications for theory. *Criminology, 26,* 591–625.

Paoline, E.A., & Terrill, W. (2007). Police education, experience, and the use of force. *Criminal Justice and Behavior, 34,* 179–196.

Pollard, J.A., Hawkins, J.D., & Arthur, M.W. (1999). Risk and protection: Are both necessary to understand diverse behavioral outcomes in adolescence? *Social Work Research, 23,* 145–158.

Piquero, A.R., Farrington, D.P., & Blumstein, A. (2003). The criminal career paradigm. In Tonry, M (ed), *Crime & Justice: A Review of Research* (vol 30), 359–506. Chicago, IL: University of Chicago Press.

Reiss, A.J. (1971). *The Police and the Public*. New Haven, CT: Yale University Press.

Rubenstein, J. (1973). *City Police*. New York: Farrar, Straus, and Giroux.

Sampson, R.J., & Laub, J.H. (1993). *Crime in the making: Pathways and turning points through life*. Cambridge, MA: Havard University Press.

Sampson, R. J., & Laub, J.H. (1996). Socioeconomic achievement in the life course of disadvantaged men: Military service as a turning point, circa 1940–1965. *American Sociological Review, 61*, 347–367.

Sampson, R.J., & Laub, J.H. (2003). Life-course desisters? Trajectories of crime among delinquent boys followed to age 70. *Criminology, 41*, 555–592.

Scrivner, E.M. (1994). *Controlling Police Use of Excessive Force: The Role of the Police Psychologist*. Washington, DC: National Institute of Justice, Research in Brief.

Shelder, J., & Block, J. (1990). Adolescent drug use and psychological health: A longitudinal inquiry. *American Psychologist, 45*, 612–630.

Sherman, L.W. (1974). *Police Corruption: A Sociological Perspective*. Garden City, NJ: Doubleday Books.

Sherman, L. W. (1975). An evaluation of policewomen on patrol in a suburban police department. *Journal of Police Science & Administration, 3*, 434–438.

Skolnick, J. (1975). *Justice Without Trial: Law Enforcement in Democratic Society* (2nd ed). New York, NY: John Wiley and Sons.

Sterling, J. W. (1972). *Changes in the Role Concepts of Police Officers*. Washington, DC: International Association of Chiefs of Police.

Sykes, R.E., & Brent, E.E. (1985). *Policing: A Social Behaviorist Perspective*. New Brunswick, NJ: Rutgers University Press.

Terrill, W., & Mastrofski, S.D. (2002). Situational and officer-based determinants of police coercion. *Justice Quarterly, 19,* 215–248.

Terrill, W., & McClusky (2002). Citizen complaints and problem officers: Examining officer behavior. *Journal of Criminal Justice,* 30, 143–155.

Toch, H (1996). The violence-prone police officer. In W. A. Geller & H. Toch (Eds.), *Understanding and Controlling Police Abuse of Force.* New Haven, CT: Yale University Press

Thornberry, T.P. (1997). Some advantages of developmental and life-course perspectives for the study of crime and delinquency. In T.P. Thornberry (Ed.), *Developmental Theories of Crime and Delinquency.* New Brunswick, NJ: Transaction Books.

Tittle, C.R. (1988). Two empirical regularities (maybe) in search of an explanation: Commentary on the age/crime debate. *Criminology, 26,* 75–85.

Van Maanen, J. (1973). Observations on the making of policemen. *Human Organizations, 32,* 407–418.

Van Maanen, J. (1974). Working the street: A developmental view of police behavior. In H. Jacob (Ed.), *The Potential for Reform of Criminal Justice.* Beverly Hills, CA: Sage.

Van Maanen, J. (1975). Police socialization: A longitudinal examination of job attitudes in an urban police department. *Administrative Science Quarterly, 20,* 207–228.

Van Maanen, J. (1978). The asshole. In P. K. Manning, & J. Van Maanen (Eds). *Policing: A View from the Street* (pp. 221–238). Santa Monica, CA: Goodyear.

Walker, S., & Bumphus, V.W. (1992). The effectiveness of civilian review: Observations on recent trends and new issues regarding the civilian review of the police. *American Journal of Police, 11,* 1–26.

Walker, S. "Minority and Female Employment in Policing: The Implications of 'Glacial' Change." *Crime & Delinquency.* 31 (1985): 555–572.

Westley, W.A. (1970). *Violence and the Police: A Sociological Study of Law, Custom, and Morality.* Cambridge, MA: MIT Press.

Whitaker, G. (1982). *Basic issues in policing.* Washington, DC: US Government Printing Office.

Wolfgang, M.E., Figlio, R., & Sellin, T. (1972). *Delinquency in a birth cohort.* Chicago: University of Chicago Press.

Worden, A.P. (1993). The attitudes of women and men in policing: Testing conventional and contemporary wisdom. *Criminology, 31,* 203–237.

Worden, R.E. (1989). Situation and attitudinal explanations of police behavior: A theoretical reappraisal and empirical assessment. *Law & Society Review, 23,* 667–711.

Worden, R.E. (1990). A badge and a baccalaureate: Policies, hypotheses, and further evidence. *Justice Quarterly, 7,* 565–592.

Worden, R.E. (1995). Police officers' belief systems: A framework for analysis. *American Journal of Police, 14,* 49–81.

Worden, R.E. (1996). The causes of police brutality: Theory and evidence on the police use of force. In W. A. Geller & H. Toch (Eds.), *Understanding and Controlling Police Abuse of Force.* New Haven, CT: Yale University Press.

Worden, R.E., & Shepard, R.L. (1996). Demeanor, crime and police behavior: A reexamination of the police services study data. *Criminology, 34,* 83–105.

Index